THE WEB BEFORE THE WEB

PUTTING THE HYPE INTO HYPERTEXT

IAN RITCHIE

COPPERTOP

First published in Great Britain in 2023

COPPERTOP
www.coppertop.co.uk

Text © Ian Ritchie, 2023

The right of Ian Ritchie to be identified as the
author of this work has been asserted by him in accordance with the
Copyright, Designs and Patents Act 1988

British Library Cataloguing-in-Publication Data
A catalogue record for this book is available on
request from the British Library

ISBN 9798866747412

Edited by Helen Bleck Editorial Services
Created in Vellum

CONTENTS

1. Opportunity?   1
2. Dalkeith Palace   5
3. The Pittsburgh PERQ   13
4. Export to Expert   27
5. OWL takes wing   42
6. Getting started   54
7. It's called 'hypertext'   76
8. Setting up in Seattle   84
9. Building a hypertext future   96
10. A bump in the road   105
11. Attracting attention   112
12. Bellevue blues   120
13. Topping up the tank   131
14. Nurturing our American OWL   135
15. A better Guide   142
16. Guidex – industrial-strength hypertext   153
17. Osaka calling   161
18. A deal is done   171
19. Turning Japanese   185
20. The cuckoo lurking in the hypertext nest   200
21. The Web takes off   211
22. Conclusion   218
23. Key timelines   222
24. Glossary   225

About the Author   231

1

OPPORTUNITY?

I t's late November 1990 and I am on the outskirts of Paris. The final leaves are dropping off the late autumn trees and I am attending a technology conference in a convention building a few metres away from the grand palace of Versailles.

I am here to attend the first European Conference on Hypertext Technology, known as 'ECHT'. There are presentations of technical and academic research papers and an associated exhibition, at which Office Workstations Limited (OWL), our company, is demonstrating our software package, Guide, the world's first commercial hypertext package.

By 1990, the world of computing has changed dramatically. A decade earlier most computing was done on mainframes, locked away in air-conditioned rooms and guarded by computer operators who knew little about the programs that they were running. Computer programs were usually input on punched cards, and output was delivered on large-format sheets printed by devices called 'line printers' which could only print fixed-space text. There were a few early personal computers such as the Apple II, but they were mostly used by hobbyists.

In 1981, IBM launched their personal computer (PC) and transformed the whole world of computation, bringing a level of corporate recognition to a form of computer that up to that time was not perceived by many as suitable for business tasks. This movement was later accelerated by the launch in 1984 of the Apple Macintosh, with its user-friendly graphics-based computing environment, a form of computer interface which was later adopted by all subsequent personal computers.

Suddenly, the world of computing was turned upside down, as users had their own computer at their personal disposal, and it created a unique opportunity to define the applications that would be needed by PC users. Wholly new applications such as word processors, spreadsheets and so on.

Our company, OWL, had been fortunate to be in the right place at the right time, and we had been responsible for developing an innovative computer publishing technology that provided documents that were intended to be read and navigated on a computer screen.

It was called hypertext.

Hypertext is the name given to 'dynamic document' software – sets of documents displayed on a screen that can be navigated by pointing to 'hot spots' with a computer mouse and clicking the mouse button. The document will then do something – most often it will open up to more information or to retrieve and display another, related, document.

This conference in Versailles is for the global hypertext community which, in 1990, is tiny – only around 250 delegates attend a gathering on such an esoteric subject.

I am approached in the corridor by a smart young man who says to me "Are you Ian Ritchie?", and when I confirm, he says, "We need to talk; let's get a beer."

In the bar, he introduces himself.

His name is Tim Berners-Lee and he tells me about a project he has been working on, off and on, for a few years. It's a basic hypertext system which he has been developing while working at the CERN (the European Laboratory for Particle Physics near Geneva). At that moment his system only existed on his NeXT computer in his office, but in a few weeks' time he plans to open it up to other users at CERN.

He has called his system the 'WorldWideWeb',[1] and designed it to allow the researchers at CERN to quickly browse and study collections of documents accessed via the internet, all interlinked so that they can quickly switch from document to document.

But his ambitions do not end there. He explains that the reason he gave it such an aspirational name is that he envisages it ultimately being used by almost everybody for their everyday communications and information sharing. I must admit that I thought this to be rather an ambitious goal for what was essentially a minor unofficial research project in a major advanced physics research centre. It was difficult to visualise the wider adoption of his technology, especially as it was based on the Internet, which at that time was only used by the research community and was not available to the wider community.

The reason he particularly wants to speak with me is that his WorldWideWeb could only display plain text. Our software package, Guide, was a sophisticated hypertext management system which displayed richly formatted documents consisting of text in different sizes and typefaces and containing embedded images, graphics and photographs.

He was looking for a browser – a smart user interface – for his WorldWideWeb and he thought we could quickly write one, as indeed we easily could have. But the internet was not widely available – it will be at least two more years before it began to be opened up for commercial use. But at that time, it was still strictly non-commercial, limited to use by individuals in government, defence or academic research. There was therefore no commercial market for such a product.

Nor could Tim offer to pay us to develop a browser, as CERN has not allocated him any budget for this project – it hadn't, yet, gained any priority at the physics research centre. As far as CERN management was concerned, their job was to research breakthroughs in particle physics, not in software. As a result, Tim had been running a 'skunk-works' project – a project with the knowledge of his manager but with no formal status or budget.

OF COURSE, it turned out that I was very wrong about the potential of Berners-Lee's WorldWideWeb. These days the World Wide Web provides the mechanism through which modern communications, publishing, broadcasting and commerce are enabled. Many would rate it as the most revolutionary communications technology since Gutenberg pioneered printing with moveable type.

Tim Berners-Lee's technology was to go on to conquer the world, but, frankly, nobody, except maybe Tim, could have known that at the time.

So, where did the core browser technology, 'hypertext' – the technology that has changed the world – come from?

This is our small contribution to that story...

---

1. His descriptive title, 'WorldWideWeb', later became the 'World Wide Web'.

2

DALKEITH PALACE

My first job in the computer industry was in the rather grand Dalkeith Palace, an elegant old mansion set in a substantial park eight miles south of Edinburgh, located at the east end of the High Street of Dalkeith, a Midlothian market town. Originally a castle, the building was remodelled in 1703 in the style of a Dutch palace, Het Loo in Apeldoorn, by Anne Scott, the Duchess of Buccleuch.

Over the centuries, Dalkeith Castle and later Palace had played significant roles in history, frequently hosting the Scottish royal family, especially when Edinburgh was struck by plague, which seemed to happen often.

James VI of Scotland was in residence at the castle in 1587 when news arrived that his mother, Mary, Queen of Scots, had been executed on the orders of Queen Elizabeth of England. Both King George IV in 1820 and Queen Victoria in 1842 based themselves at Dalkeith Palace on their respective first visits to Scotland.

Dalkeith Palace

The Buccleuch family stopped using Dalkeith Palace as a residence just before the First World War and the building had been largely empty until the late 1960s when it was leased as offices by International Computers Limited (ICL), then the leading British computer manufacturer.

ICL had been formed in the 1960s at the instigation of the UK Labour Government. Tony Benn, the Minister for Industry, encouraged mergers between all the early computing businesses in the UK – companies like English Electric, Elliott, LEO, Ferranti, Marconi and ICT were eventually encouraged to form ICL in order to create a competitive computer company capable of trading on a global scale.

In the 1970s ICL became one of the so-called 'Seven Dwarfs' of the computer industry, where Snow White was represented by the industry leader IBM; the other Dwarfs were the likes of Honeywell, Burroughs, RCA . . . and ICL.

ICL was the biggest computer company outside the USA

and had a particularly strong customer base in the UK public sector, and in the countries of the old British Commonwealth such as India, Africa, Australia and New Zealand. It had also managed to secure business in Russia and Eastern Europe where US Cold War sanctions had limited the sale of advanced American computing technology.

In those days the UK government had an interventionist attitude to technology companies and one of the many pressures exerted on ICL was that they should set up a new research and development (R&D) centre somewhere in the north of the UK to spread skilled jobs throughout the country. As there were already strong research links with the University of Edinburgh, they looked for suitable premises nearby, and thus the rather grand but somewhat dilapidated Dalkeith Palace was chosen.

It was a sublime location in which to develop computer software. We programmers worked in wood-panelled rooms with marble fireplaces carved by Grinling Gibbons, underneath old masters by Claude Lorrain and Rubens. A majestic life-size marble statue of the Duke of Wellington kept a watch over us at the bottom of an impressive, main staircase.

This was my first job on leaving university and my starting salary, in July 1973, was £1,430 a year.

This was also the time I got married. I had known my wife, Barbara, from school, but we had waited until we had both graduated and started working before tying the knot. Barbara had been awarded a First Class Honours degree in Mathematics and Physics from the University of Edinburgh, and was starting a career as a tax inspector in Edinburgh. Six years later, in 1980, while I was still at Dalkeith Palace, Barbara gave birth to our son, Niall.

The Dalkeith Palace part of ICL was the smallest R&D office in the group, and there was always a feeling that they didn't quite know what to do with us. We were variously given responsibility for maintaining operating systems and their range of communications processors, and we made a speciality of emulation systems, the art of making new computers work exactly like the old ones so that customers could run all their legacy software, ideally without having to change anything.

Roughly 100 people worked at Dalkeith Palace and, as most of the staff were young graduates, romantic entanglements and other social activities flourished: games of croquet on the back lawn, treasure hunts around the neighbourhood, volunteer trips for local disadvantaged kids and so on. Many people would exercise in the grounds at lunchtime; except on Wednesdays, when we were warned that the Buccleuch gamekeepers were armed and inclined to 'cull' some of the pheasants that they farmed – and potentially shoot any software engineer who accidentally got in their way.

My first job was one of the team responsible for the 'J' operating system for the ICL System 4, an IBM 360-compatible machine made under licence from the US company RCA (the RCA Spectra range). This was, at that time, the largest computer made by ICL and I recall one day a discussion with our marketing colleagues about whether we should extend the addressing limits of the machine from the then current eight megabytes to 16 megabytes. Although we could not really envisage such a number being needed, the decision was finally taken to future-proof it and extend the addressable memory to 32 megabytes.

Today, of course, it is perfectly normal to have more than a thousand times that amount of memory (multiple gigabytes in fact) in the phone you carry in your pocket.

Those were the days when a lunchtime visit to the pub was fairly normal, especially on a Friday, when many of the employees routinely decamped to the nearest bar, the Greyhound, just outside the Palace gates. One particular Friday the local pub had installed a novel new attraction – an arcade game

– and many of us put our 10p in the slot and played a game of Space Invaders, an early arcade game where the object was to destroy waves of aliens before one of them dropped a bomb on you. Back in those days the UK licensing laws meant that the pub was required to close at 2.30pm, so we were limited to the four pints or so that could be downed during our extended lunch break.

One still wonders about the quality of the software written on Friday afternoons following these outings, but one particular member of our group decidedly demonstrated that he, at least, had remained level-headed.

This was David Corner, a quiet-spoken bearded lad who came from Thurso, a small town on the most northerly coast of Scotland. David had come south to study Physics at the University of Edinburgh and had joined ICL at Dalkeith as a software engineer, a role at which he excelled. Between 2.30pm, when we all staggered back from the pub, and 5pm that afternoon, when we were all drifting off for the weekend, he had created an accurate clone of Space Invaders on one of the communications computers in our office, complete with left/right and firing buttons, and generating noises when the aliens were eliminated, or when the player, inevitably, met his fate.

If nothing else, it saved us all a lot of 10p stakes at the pub.

In 1977, ICL's business performance was not good and a new Managing Director was appointed, again after intervention by the UK government. Dr Chris Wilson arrived from the oil company BP as our proposed saviour, and before long he arrived at Dalkeith to give us a pep talk and rally the troops.

In the final year of my university computer science course, I had completed an individual project on a Digital Equipment PDP8. The PDP stood for 'Personal Data Processor' and it was one of the earliest opportunities to have a dedicated computer under your own control.

It wasn't really a personal computer as we know it today –

input was achieved by punching instructions onto fan-fold paper tape, and output was sent to a noisy, clattering, teletype printer. Still, it was my 'personal' computer, as long as I was sitting in front of it.

I became quickly sold on the concept of 'personal computing' and eagerly followed any developments in this field. One day, I was sure, the personal computer would become ubiquitous.

So, when it came to the Q&A session with our new CEO Chris Wilson, I stuck up my hand.

"I've noticed," I said, "that Dixons – the high street electrical retailer – have started selling the Commodore PET personal computer, and that businesses are starting to buy these machines to manage their administration tasks. Does ICL intend to get involved at this entry-level part of our business?"

He looked down his nose at me. "ICL doesn't make toys," he said.

Well – that was me put in my place.

The very next day I was off to ICL's Manchester hardware development centre, located in the city's district of West Gorton. Frankly, this wasn't the best part of that city; it was the location later chosen for the setting of Channel 4's *Shameless*, a TV drama series about a dysfunctional single father raising six children, who spends his days drunk or on the edge of criminal activities, while his children largely take care of themselves.

The reason I was at West Gorton was for our fortnightly progress report on the development of the largest and most powerful new computer that ICL had ever made. It was called the ICL 2966, and based on the MU5 processor design developed at the University of Manchester.

One of the features of this computer design was that it could be altered, by rewriting its microcode, to perform as a different machine. We could, for example, reprogram it to work exactly like the ICL System 4 computer, which had been widely used, among others, by the UK Post Office.

I led a team at Dalkeith developing a System 4 emulation system for this machine that would allow the UK Post Office, among others, to be the first customer to use this new computer without having to change any of the software or operational practices on their, by now, obsolete System 4 machines. If they were happy with the performance, they had committed to buying 20 of these new computers – quite a lucrative order for ICL – and, as a result, our project had gained a fairly high-priority status in the company.

In this design office, where they were responsible for creating what, at the time, was ICL's most powerful ever computer and as a result they had access to as much computing power as they could reasonably want, I noticed a small type-writer-sized device in one of the side offices.

"What's that?" I asked.

"Oh, that's an Apple II," I was told. "We're using VisiCalc on it to run the budget and coordinate the plans for the 2966 development." VisiCalc was the first spreadsheet program and one of the first 'killer apps' – a software package which on its own is so valuable it justifies the purchase of the computer.

In the words of Chris Wilson though, this was 'a toy'.

But it was the right toy, the tool for the job, and as it proved, personal computers did have a great future, even if the then Managing Director of ICL couldn't envisage it.

And I wanted to be part of it – my order had gone in for a BBC Micro, an innovative early personal computer which had been selected to support a broadcast educational campaign mounted by the UK national broadcaster BBC and which had been designed and developed by a young start-up company – Acorn Computers of Cambridge.

When it eventually arrived, I noted with some irony that my

BBC Micro had been actually manufactured by ICL in one of their factories.

It was certainly an innovative personal computer, and it was an early example of what was to go on to become the future shape of computing technology, but ICL was yet to engage with these developments.

Chris Wilson didn't last much longer at ICL.

3

THE PITTSBURGH PERQ

ICL was once again in crisis by 1981 and had to be bailed out by the UK government. This time it was decided that an executive called Robb Wilmot, who although UK-born had made a name for himself as a highly effective young Vice-President at the USA's Texas Instruments company (TI), should be installed as the new CEO. Wilmot, accompanied by his TI sidekick Peter Bonfield, immediately set about shaking up ICL.

A few initiatives had already been set in motion. One, with somewhat of a sense of panic about it, was that ICL should urgently investigate catching up with the competition and develop a personal computer. Samir Sinawi and I were assigned to investigate what had been dubbed by management as an 'Apple Eater' project, aimed to – belatedly – compete against the Apple II. Samir was a world-class system designer, originally from Kurdistan in northern Iraq, who after his career at ICL went on to join the faculty at the Massachusetts Institute of Technology (MIT).

We received a shipment of what ICL thought might be a good candidate for their PC – a communications processor which was built into a large metal-framed full desk-sized 'work-station'. Watching the workmen struggling to manipulate this equipment up a narrow staircase in the venerable Dalkeith Palace we were somewhat unconvinced that this system could be easily repackaged into a small personal computer to compete with the machines being made by Apple, Commodore, Exidy Sorcerer, Texas Instruments etc.

In any case, also in 1981, the IBM PC was launched, and the credibility carried by the mighty IBM transformed the whole personal computer scene overnight. ICL couldn't just play at this anymore with small 'skunk work' projects. The 'Apple Eater' project was quickly wound up.

ALL OF TODAY'S modern personal computers, indeed all its successor devices such as today's smartphones and tablets, are based on what is known as a graphical user interface (GUI), based on a display of 'windows' on which you can view different applications incorporating sophisticated layouts, type-faces and images, and actions are triggered either by a pointing device such as a computer 'mouse' or in modern handheld devices by touching the screen. But early personal computers, such as the IBM PC and the Apple II were not at all like this – they had fixed text spacing like a basic typewriter and were relatively poor at displaying graphics or images. Video was completely out of the question.

The first commercially released computer to be launched anywhere in the world which was based on a graphical user interface – the type of computing that has since become very familiar to anyone using an Apple Macintosh or Microsoft Windows system – was called the PERQ, and was developed by a start-up Pittsburgh company, Three Rivers Computer Corporation (3RCC), named after the three rivers which come together in that city: the Allegheny and the Monongahela which join together and flow out as the Ohio. It was a spin-out company based on designs undertaken at Pittsburgh's Carnegie Mellon, the university based in that city which had developed an excellent reputation for advanced computing research.

The Carnegie Mellon engineers had also been influenced by the work done throughout the 1970s in California at Stanford University and at the nearby Xerox PARC (Palo Alto Research Centre) in developing a conceptual machine called the Xerox Alto; the Alto was the machine which, when later demonstrated to Steve Jobs, inspired him to go ahead and build most of these features into the creation of the Apple Macintosh.

Although owned by the mighty Xerox corporation, Xerox PARC was renowned for both its phenomenal research achievements and the company's puzzling inability to manage to commercialise any of its technology breakthroughs.

One of the founders [HB1] of the PERQ, Brian Rosen, had moved from Pittsburgh to California to work at PARC but, frustrated at the lack of any sign of commercial progress there, had returned to 3RCC to re-join his colleagues and bring the PERQ to market.

The PERQ

THE PERQ WAS LAUNCHED at the world's leading graphics computing conference, ACM SIGGRAPH in August 1979, which that year was held in Chicago, and the very first sale completed by 3RCC was to the UK's Rutherford Appleton Laboratory (RAL), the body which determined the research priorities for physical and mathematical sciences in the UK.

The Rutherford Laboratory had decided that the PERQ was their favoured choice for use in all personal scientific computing research in UK universities, and they committed to buying an initial 10 computers from 3RCC. They then persuaded ICL to take these US-manufactured machines and convert them for safe use in the UK.

One of Robb Wilmot's early conclusions when he arrived as the new ICL CEO was that the company could not do everything by itself, and that it should be more willing to partner with other companies to provide a full range of computing products for a variety of different needs. Although, at $10,000 or so, the PERQ wasn't targeted at the $2,000 price tag typical of the consumer PC market, it was still a breakthrough powerful computer for personal use by professionals.

It didn't take long for Wilmot's ICL to agree to a partnership deal with 3RCC to add this advanced graphics workstation to ICL's range of products, encouraged by the enthusiasm shown by RAL to buy more of these computers for UK academic researchers.

The PERQ, for its time, was an impressive feat of computer engineering with a very high-resolution black and white 300 dots per inch (dpi) page-size screen capable of displaying fast, complex graphics.

Unfortunately, the software installed on the machine was not up to the same standards, which became a priority for us at ICL.

This development looked ideal to be run at Dalkeith Palace, as it was a relatively small, self-contained project, and made the most of the advanced computing skills that we already had at Dalkeith. We were also based near, and had good relations with, the University of Edinburgh, which had the largest computer science research department in the UK.

Our task was to improve the software offerings of this machine. Rather than adopting the increasingly standard Unix operating system, 3RCC had developed the PERQ with a non-standard Pascal-based operating system and as a result it could only run a limited range of applications.

At Dalkeith Palace we had skills in operating systems, languages and networking. Our main role in this partnership was to help the PERQ become a more comprehensive and effective all-round offering.

It was decided that I was to be put in charge of running the ICL end of the PERQ project. I had been promoted regularly in my first six years at ICL and by now was seen by management as an effective technology manager.

My job would be to manage the project at Dalkeith, which would develop a range of operating systems and computer languages for the PERQ, and to act as the main liaison between ICL and the 3RCC company.

And so it was that I found myself one day sitting in Heathrow Terminal 3 waiting for a TWA flight to Pittsburgh. This was the first time I had ever visited the USA and I was excited. I was accompanied by Roger Ashbrooke, the Bracknell-based ICL manager who had been the caretaker manager looking after the project until that point.

As it turned out, Pittsburgh in the early 1980s wasn't an ideal location for my first introduction to the United States. It was a classic 'rust belt' city and the outskirts of town seemed to be peppered by huge derelict heavy engineering manufacturing plants which had been closed and abandoned. Its easy access to local supplies of coal and iron ore had, in past times, led Pittsburgh to become the heart of the US steel industry, and it had made Andrew Carnegie, the steel magnate, the richest man in the world.

Those days, however, were long past; it was now decidedly post-industrial, and Pittsburgh was trying to reinvent itself under the optimistic brand of the 'Renaissance City'.

It was Andrew Carnegie, originally from Dunfermline in Scotland, who founded the Institute of Technology in 1912 which had later grown into Carnegie Mellon University (CMU), which had one of the strongest computer science research centres in the world, and were the originators of the PERQ.

The large old red brick building in North Craig Street where 3RCC was based had once been a mill, but had now been reborn as the home of this start-up high-tech computer company. In front of the building was a large car park and on the other side of this was a railway line where extremely long freight trains frequently trundled past.

The Pittsburgh company was much stronger in designing hardware than developing software and so we in our ICL team largely took on the load of commissioning a much-needed Unix operating system for the PERQ and adding various computer languages such as Fortran and C.

Over the next few weeks, Ashbrooke withdrew, and I became the main liaison, both with Three Rivers and with Carnegie Mellon. I visited Pittsburgh every six weeks or so, staying at the University Inn, a modest business hotel on Forbes Avenue.

As well as the 3RCC partnership, ICL was also interested in a possible relationship with Carnegie Mellon University, and so I began investigating signing up as a partner in their SPICE project,[1] an advanced operating system research initiative consisting of a group of researchers under the direction of Raj Reddy, who was such a distinguished scientist that he was later awarded the prestigious Turing Award, the world's highest recognition for computer science researchers.

SPICE was addressing the technical issues arising in implementing modern distributed operating systems, which run across networks of computers, and the various other companies that were already members of this club were virtually a who's-who of the computer industry: Hewlett-Packard, IBM, DEC, Apple, Microsoft and so on.

I was also intrigued by another major project that was

underway at CMU at that time: ZOG, an early interactive documentation system which was intended to be installed on a
network of PERQs on the proposed 'paper-free' naval ship, the
USS *Carl Vinson*. The *Carl Vinson*, which was then under
construction for the US Navy, was to be the largest aircraft
carrier in the world when completed. Long corridors of offices
in CMU seemed to be dedicated to this project; I was amazed at
the sheer quantity of defence funding that was being spent on
what was still essentially early-stage academic computing
research.

The deployment of ZOG on the USS *Carl Vinson* was later
reported to have failed in enabling the carrier to effectively
operate paper-free but Rob Akscyn and Donald McCracken,
the two leaders of the ZOG project, later founded a commercial
follow-on company called Knowledge Management System Inc
(KMS), which was to become one of the significant players
among the emerging hypertext research community.

There were two-day technical briefings held twice a year in
which developments in the SPICE projects were communi-
cated to members of this club and Peter Hibbard, an
Englishman who was the gatekeeper of the SPICE project at
Carnegie Mellon, was keen that ICL should join up as a
member. I was invited as a guest to the next partners' briefing
session and told that the membership bill was $50,000 a year
should we want to join.

The briefing session was fascinating, and it seemed to me
that it was important that we should sign up. Indeed, many of
the features and techniques that they were then pioneering
have later become embedded in today's Microsoft Windows
and Apple's Mac OS X.

I reported back to my masters in ICL the importance of this
work and the company that we would be keeping. I was told
that my negotiation skills were clearly pathetic, that $50,000

was a rip off, and that the matter would be pursued at a more senior level.

So, a few months later when Robb Wilmot decided to visit CMU and 3RCC, I assumed my other role of 'bag carrier' to our CEO. He was offhand, I thought quite perfunctory, particularly towards Reddy, despite the considerable reputation he held among the computing community. Ultimately, Wilmot met with Hibbard to set the price of our membership, which he finally agreed at $50,000.

So much for my poor negotiation skills.

We continued our strong relationship with the Rutherford Laboratory, who had been responsible for most of the initial purchases of the ICL PERQ. One of the sockets on the PERQ was an RS232 serial port, suitable for driving various peripherals such as printers and graphics plotters, but the firmware to drive this port hadn't been written. As this was part of the standard PERQ hardware offering it was clearly the responsibility of 3RCC.

I raised this issue at my next review meeting at 3RCC. They maintained that although there was indeed a physical RS232 port on the machine, it was driven by a Z80 processor chip and that they maintained that they had absolutely no Z80 skills within their company. I'd done my share of microprocessor programming in the past and I knew full well that if you could program one type of microprocessor, you could quickly adapt to a different one given the specification sheet, however, they were adamant that it was impossible for them to do this task in a timely manner and that they were completely unable to deliver.

I also knew that it was really a relatively simple task and, indeed, I had in mind a programmer back at Dalkeith who was very experienced in communications systems and who could almost certainly complete it in a few days; I also knew that he had been experimenting in his own time with a Z80-based microcomputer hobby kit.

I gave in. Our marketing people had insisted that the RS232 was required, so if 3RCC wasn't willing to do it, we would do it ourselves.

My formal morning meetings completed; I did what I often did at 3RCC – I 'wandered around'. The company was very undisciplined, and I often found valuable information from chatting to individual employees, the people actually designing and developing their computers.

As I was walking down one of the large corridors of the old mill building, I heard a singing voice coming from the other side of one of the large wooden doors. Someone or something was singing: 'I wish I were in Dixie, Hurray, Hurray'.

I opened the door, and at the far corner of a large, high-ceilinged room was an individual sitting at a PERQ, and his computer was lustily singing 'I wish I were in Dixie, Hurray, Hurray'. I asked the engineer what he was up to. He explained that he had discovered that there was a loudspeaker driven by a Z80 processor in the PERQ, and that if you programmed it correctly you could make it sing.

So much for their lack of Z80 skills.

THREE RIVERS COMPUTER was a typical chaotic start-up company and as such suffered from regular management crises. One week in 1982 while I was in their Pittsburgh office in the old mill building, I learned that the VP Technology and VP Marketing had both been fired and I bumped into the VP Human Resources in the corridor who complained he had no idea what was going on – he was also gone by the end of that week.

Ed Friedkin, an MIT professor who had been an early

investor in the company and had been the founding Chairman, along with Jim Gay, whom he had hired as President in January 1981, both resigned, to be replaced by Richard Rifenburgh as Chairman and Aaron Coleman as President. A second HQ and development centre was set up near Boston and it soon became the centre of decision-making for the company, as the new management team preferred to work in the high-tech Boston area where it was much easier to hire and retain skilled high tech staff than in rust-belt Pittsburgh.

Another summit meeting between 3RCC and ICL was arranged, to be held at the Boston Park Plaza Hotel, a grand old edifice facing onto Boston Common. I was once again required to assume my, by now familiar, role as ICL bag-carrier for Wilmot, my presence again was barely noticed.

After flying in from the UK in the late afternoon before the next morning's meeting I decided to try and get some fresh air after dinner, and I went out from the Boston Park Plaza Hotel for a wander around the town. This turned out to be a bad idea. The city centre, which was normally packed with people through the day, was eerily quiet in the evening. As I walked along the empty streets there was nobody around except a few shadowy figures in doorways that made me feel uncomfortable. Eventually I rounded a corner and came across a couple of streets that turned out to be Boston's red-light district, known locally as the 'Combat Zone'. That was quite a relief – not only was it relatively busy with lots of people around, but there were also police cars on all the corners. From there it was a short sprint back to my hotel.

After a traditional first night of jet-lagged, disturbed sleep, I woke up in my room at the Park Plaza and switched on the TV breakfast news: 'STABBING LAST NIGHT AT THE BOSTON PARK PLAZA HOTEL!' screamed the local news programme, along with footage of an unfortunate victim being wheeled out of the hotel – *this* hotel – on a paramedic's trolley.

Welcome to metropolitan USA.

MY COUPLE of years running the PERQ project introduced me
to a whole new set of life skills. I had managed to fit in some
free time visiting the sights of New York, Boston and Washington DC, sat perplexed through a game of American football,
learned how to drive an automatic car, and fallen in love with
the superb bookshops and branches of Tower Records that
were located in the university districts of American cities.

I had seen at first hand a start-up company which had spun
out of a university research lab become a notable global player,
taking on the world with its innovative technology, and I had
developed a taste for the US high-tech scene and its fast-
emerging personal computer revolution.

For a lad brought up in a working-class village in central
Scotland – my father had left school at 14 to take a job for life as
a shale miner – I had become a small cog in the transatlantic
machine of innovative computing technology business. One
thing was for sure: there was no going back.

I had really enjoyed my years at ICL Dalkeith. I had gained
enormous experience of running complex computer development projects, and I thought that running the PERQ project
was the best job in the whole company, but I could also see that
it couldn't, and it wouldn't, last. Having had several great jobs
throughout my years at Dalkeith, eventually running what,
although relatively small, was one of the most exciting and
high-profile projects in the company, my next job within ICL
would undoubtedly require me to move away from Dalkeith.

The choices within ICL weren't attractive: Bracknell in
Berkshire or Kidsgove in Staffordshire were the other two software R&D centres, and my dealings so far with the two divi-
sional Directors who ran these operations had been singularly

unimpressive. My next job would almost certainly involve reporting directly to one of those two individuals.

I was contacted by Sandy Blackie, who had run ICL Dalkeith for several years. He had a proposition – he had joined up with a wealthy New York-based individual, Seymour Joffe, known as Sy, who had agreed to fund a new start-up company to take UK software to the US market using his network of connections in the US technology scene. Sandy proposed that I join him as Technical Director of this company, where I would lead a search for suitable UK-developed software technology, which we then would package up to sell to the fast-growing emerging personal computer market in the States.

It seemed like an exciting opportunity and I agreed to join him.

When I handed in my notice to Chris Barfield, the then manager of ICL Dalkeith, he was clearly disappointed. My hope that my notice period could be shortened was quickly dashed and I was required to work out my full three months' notice. Another young rising star within ICL, Peter Palmer, was quickly identified to take over from me and he relocated up to Dalkeith from the Bracknell office to take over responsibility for the PERQ project.

The new company that I joined was to be called Export Software International (ESI) and was initially based in Sandy's house in South Oswald Road in the Grange, a leafy area of southern Edinburgh.

~

IN THE END, the PERQ didn't survive. The company changed its name from 3RCC to PERQ System Corporation in 1984 but it then went bust in 1986. Although well engineered, the PERQ never quite got its software act together. Like many other pioneering companies, it had been overtaken by later, better,

IAN RITCHIE

more powerful graphic workstations, in this case from Apollo (which was bought by Hewlett-Packard), and Silicon Graphics, but most of all by the phenomenally successful SUN Computer Systems, a spin-out from Stanford University, at the heart of Silicon Valley.

---

1. SPICE stood for 'Software Process Improvement and Capability dEtermination'

4

EXPORT TO EXPERT

When I finally joined Sandy Blackie at Export Software International (ESI) we set about finding interesting bits of technology that we could package up for selling to the then strongly emerging US personal computer market. The Scottish Development Agency (SDA), a government economic development body, were helpful and provided us with useful support in identifying and marketing such technology.

The IBM PC had been launched in 1981 and had shipped with an operating system (OS) from Microsoft called MS-DOS. This was a 16-bit OS based on the same structure as the 8-bit CP/M OS that had preceded it. The creators of CP/M, Digital Research, had originally been asked by IBM to supply the OS for their PC but had failed to complete the deal. Their founder, Gary Kildall, had gone off to fly his plane and wasn't available to meet with the IBM executives. As a result, the IBM team went up to Seattle and contracted with Microsoft for the MS-DOS OS. Once they realised their miscalculation Digital Research had developed a competitor operating system for IBM PC's Intel 8086-based computer, called CP/M-86.

We came across a software developer called Mike Turner. Mike was from Birmingham but after taking his family on holiday to the Isle of Mull off the west coast of Scotland, had fallen so much in love with the place he had decided to move there.

Mike had been a jobbing software developer for many years and had developed several projects for customers based on CP/M systems. With the arrival of MS-DOS and CP/M-86 he set about writing a set of tools to help with the conversion of existing CP/M programs to the new 16-bit environment. He then set out to create other tools that were used to make developing software for the IBM PC much more efficient.

We decided to package up Turner's toolset, calling it CP/M 86 Toolbox and encouraged him to quickly develop a matching set of tools for Microsoft's OS called MS-DOS Toolbox. The personal computer was really taking off and the fact that the mighty IBM had launched their PC had given it respectability for business use. There were a growing army of developers creating applications for companies and we thought our 'Toolbox' would appeal to them.

We decided to launch our system at the January CPM-83 Conference at San Francisco's Moscone Centre. This was my first opportunity to experience the entrepreneurial climate of Northern California, the home of Silicon Valley, the world's centre of computer innovation, and the heart of the personal computer revolution.

The SDA offered to help us with shipping our exhibition stand to their US office and we flew to San Francisco and checked into our hotel, the Golden Gate Hotel Inn on the corner of Van Ness and California. We knew the SDA office was also located on California Street, so we set out the next morning, on a beautiful, sunny, cloudless day, to walk to it. Little did we know it was a very long street indeed and, being in San

Francisco, also required a fair bit of climbing, up the road and then down the other side.

Finally, we arrived and met with Jimmy Reid, who ran the local SDA office. We were there to pick up our exhibition stand materials, but we were surprised to discover that they hadn't arrived. A few phone calls were made, and it transpired that our exhibition materials had been shipped to the SDA's main US office in Connecticut, near New York, on the other side of the continent.

And so it was that at the crack of dawn the next morning – the day the show opened – we drove to the freight depot at San Francisco airport to pick up our exhibition materials, which had been emergency-shipped from Connecticut. We then dashed directly to the Moscone Centre in downtown San Francisco to set up in time for the show to open at 10am. We made it, but only just.

It turned out to be a good show for us. Digital Research was, at that time, still a major force in the industry as more people were still using CP/M on 8-bit machines than had so far switched to the new 16-bit PCs. And we were well received – it was full of developers who were facing opportunities in the new 16-bit world, and there seemed to be a lot of interest in our Toolbox.

One of the things that we picked up from those we spoke with was that there was real concern about piracy. Many people who bought original software packages were simply copying the master disks and passing these copies on to others. As a result, there were often many people using a software package sold for the use of the one legal purchaser.

There was clearly a real demand if we could develop an effective anti-piracy system.

I contacted David Corner, the quiet computer whizz kid who had written the Space Invaders knock-off at Dalkeith. He had a think and quickly came up with a neat solution.

In those days, software packages were normally delivered on floppy disks. A disk had to be formatted before it could be used and as it was formatted, the system would create the tracks on which the data was later to be recorded.

Between the end and the beginning of any particular track there would be a gap which varied in size from track to track and disk to disk. What David Corner did was to measure the length of several of these gaps, do a simple calculation on these values creating a unique figure, and record it somewhere else secretly on the disk.

If the content of the disk was then copied to another new disk, the formatting process would vary, and the gaps between each track would measure differently from the original; the stored hashed value would not match the one on the new disk, and it could be rejected as a copy.

We paid David £5,000 for this work and launched it under the brand name 'CopyLock'.

We then concluded an exclusive deal for this system with the Dysan Corporation, which had developed their own new format of disks and disk drives which they hoped would become a standard with the new-generation PCs. The deal was that they were licensed to protect up to one million disks per month using Copy-Lock and agreed to pay an initial advance of royalties of $250,000.

As it happens, their new disk format didn't succeed – it wasn't widely adopted by PC manufacturers – however, we had received our initial advance and we were free, after an exclusive period, to sell the program on to other customers.

Not a bad profit on a £5,000 project.

My boss, Sandy Blackie, decided that this was such a great result that his next trip to the States would be on Concorde – a decision that was thankfully reassessed as soon as he saw the astronomical price of the ticket.

On a later trip to Silicon Valley to follow up with various

business contacts, Sandy and I had our accommodation all booked but at the last minute we found that we needed to take a meeting in downtown San Francisco before heading down to the Valley, and we needed a hotel for the first night.

There was a display board in the arrival area at San Francisco airport with panels listing various hotels. A phone handset was provided and if you pressed a button next to a particular hotel you were automatically connected to their front desk. I selected one described as being on Union Square – I knew enough about San Francisco to know that Union Square was the central part of the city, the area with the upmarket stores like Louis Vuitton and Tiffany's. They confirmed that they had two rooms available, and I booked them, but just as I was hanging up the hotel receptionist said 'and that will be $34 a night'.

Oops – I thought that seemed remarkably cheap.

When we got to the hotel on Post Street it was indeed just a stone's throw from Union Square, but it could have been on a different planet. The whole place smelt like it had just been fumigated and seemed to be occupied by a remarkable number of sailors and young ladies. Our rooms hadn't been redecorated for many years and when you opened a cupboard containing a washbasin it disturbed many cockroaches, which quickly scampered off into the cracks.

That was when we discovered that cities in the States move very quickly from upmarket to downmarket districts.

By this time, we had moved our operation into our first office in central Edinburgh – a Victorian primary school, renamed Canongate Ventures, in New Street, behind the main Waverley railway station. Although it was only a few yards from the city's historic Royal Mile it wasn't a particularly attractive street. Immediately across the road was a massive ugly brick-built bus depot, which had been described in Nikolaus Pevs-

ner's standard architectural guidebook for Edinburgh as 'completely devoid of any architecture'.

Robbie McLaren joined ESI from ICL. Robbie had been a
Computer Science graduate who had led a complex software
engineering project for me at ICL and had also shown an apti-
tude for business development. It also happened that he was
'quick on the draw' and regularly amused us with his informal
cartoons.

One of Sandy Blackie's initiatives was to hire, as a consultant, Tommy Thomas and we met with him for an hour or so
once a month. Tommy had been at the birth of the modern
computer age, being one of Freddie Williams and Tom
Kilburn's team in the late 1940s at the University of Manchester.
This team had achieved in 1948 the world's first computer with
a stored program capability, which was known as the
Manchester 'Baby'.

These days, Tommy ran the Computer Services Department at the University of Edinburgh and was very well
connected in the UK computing scene, particularly in research
and advanced computing projects. He had ensured that Edinburgh had won the role of housing the most powerful high-
performance computers in the UK, which were run on behalf
of the entire UK academic research community – a role that
continues to this day – and he had also been part of the investigating trips to the USA which had led to the UK research
community adopting the PERQ.

He introduced us to Professor Donald Michie, who ran one
of the few Artificial Intelligence (AI) departments in the world
at that time. Typically for Edinburgh, they had their own name
for it: they called it Machine Intelligence.

Back in 1971 the UK Science Research Council had commissioned Sir James Lighthill to examine the prospects for AI in
UK research priorities. His report, published in 1973, poured
buckets of cold water on the discipline, which he judged was

unlikely to lead to much in the way of useful developments. This resulted in what became known in the UK as the 'AI Winter', and resulted in the closure of many AI research projects in UK universities.

To their credit, the University of Edinburgh continued to support their own Machine Intelligence department, which had been founded by Michie and Richard Gregory in the early 1960s. A small team of researchers continued to develop interesting AI research areas in Edinburgh.

I discovered later that Donald Michie had been one of the wartime code breakers at Bletchley Park, famous for breaking the German 'Enigma' code. Michie had worked with Alan Turing, Max Newman and Jack Good on breaking the much more complex coding system, the almost impenetrable 'Tunny' code, used exclusively for the most secret messages by Hitler's high command. All of this remained a closely guarded secret until around 1986, when finally, 40 years after the end of the war, they were released from the strict vow of secrecy they had all signed up to during the Second World War.

When Donald was freed to talk about it, he told me that he and Alan Turing had often played chess together, largely because although they were good players, they were not at 'grand master' level, and it was impossible for them to compete with Bletchley's best, who were genuine international standard chess 'grand masters'.

He told me a story about his friendship with Alan Turing. By 1940, Turing was convinced that Britain was going to lose the war and was worried that his wealth would be confiscated by the invading Germans. He had turned a significant portion of his personal fortune into silver and he and Donald Michie set out one day to bury the silver, ready to be dug up after hostilities were over. This they did, but when the war was over, they searched for the buried silver, but it was not to be found. The Turing hoard remains undiscovered to this day, possibly buried under one of the buildings or roundabouts in the new town of Milton Keynes, which has since been built around the town of Bletchley.

Michie showed us one of the projects that his department had been working on based on the 'ID3' algorithm, first developed by an Australian researcher called Ross Quinlan, which took a large dataset of factors and automatically created the smallest algorithm that was consistent with all the criteria fed into it. It was a kind of automated Occam's Razor, a model which states that the simplest solution to a complex problem is invariably the best one. The resulting algorithm – the smallest one that was consistent with all the data fed into it – could then be used to predict future behaviour based on past performance.

We were impressed with the power of ID3 but the interface was difficult to use. What we needed was an easy-to-use user interface for the system.

We decided to mimic the interface developed by VisiCalc for spreadsheets, where the user defined their own columns representing various factors and the result, and then populated a grid with appropriate values for each factor and the final result. Once the dataset had been set, the program automatically developed a formula that met all the criteria. This could then be used to predict various behaviours, such as in machine maintenance, economic forecasting or market behaviour.

We packaged up this product and called it Expert-Ease. We commissioned one of our fellow tenants at Canongate Ventures, a book-binder, to create a distinctive leather-bound packaging for our product in the style of an antique book. The resulting package really stood out among the standard cardboard boxes of our competitors.

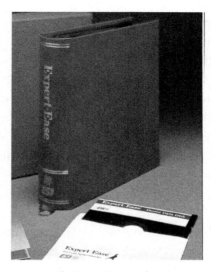

The Expert-Ease product

It attracted quite a lot of attention as it was the first example of an AI program that anybody could use on their PCs. It earned many complimentary reviews in the US trade press, with comments such as 'Expert-Ease is a very important program', in *SOFT Magazine*; 'It will probably earn its place in the history of computer science', in *Software Magazine*; and 'One of the most interesting, thought-provoking programs to come along in some time', in *PC Magazine*. This product became so significant that we decided to focus our business around it, and we even changed the name of our company from 'Export Software International' to 'Expert Software International'.

This was the first time we were able to experience being responsible for the launch of a wholly new software product category, a unique opportunity presented by the fast-growing personal computer industry. We were creating solutions that were genuinely innovative, allowing individuals to manipulate information in new and powerful ways.

The product was launched in November 1983 and we set about looking for marketing opportunities. Sandy and I

decided to attend Comdex '83, the massive computer conference and trade show held in Las Vegas. This was by far the
biggest event that I had ever attended – a massive exhibition
spread across the various huge Las Vegas hotels: the Sands,
the Hilton, Caesar's Palace and so on. We checked into the
MGM Grand Hotel, which seemed to be the size of a sizeable
town and walked what seemed like miles to our room. We
adopted the normal 'economy' Comdex approach of sharing a
large room between us; it contained two queen sized beds, and
so it was that I ended up in the room along with Sandy
Blackie.

The gambling opportunities of Las Vegas didn't appeal to
me, but Sandy went down after dinner to play the tables. He
returned around 1am having, he claimed, just won around
$10,000.

He quickly went back downstairs to play the tables again,
where, inevitably he lost the lot.

Comdex '83 was the first Comdex to have Bill Gates give the
opening speech, which became a fixed tradition in later years.
The Microsoft CEO had come down to Las Vegas, accompanied
by his father carrying a carousel of his 35mm slides, which he
then operated while his son gave the speech in the large theatre
at the Aladdin resort. Gates has never been an inspirational
speaker, and subsequent Comdex opening speeches were
enlivened by elaborately produced videos created by Microsoft
to sharpen up his presentations.

Part of Gates's speech covered his vision of the future,
including very early indications about Microsoft Windows, a
future system for the PC which he predicted would use a
graphical user interface and be operated using a computer
mouse.

There were other nascent windowing systems on view at
the show, including VisiOn from the publishers of VisiCalc, a
product called DesqView from a company called Quarterdeck,

and a demonstration of a mouse-driven system developed for an Apple II.

One contact I picked up at Comdex was a senior executive at Microsoft called Alan Boyd. Boyd was a Scot who he had lived in the USA for 15 years or so. He had taken part in an exchange programme to the States while studying for a Physics degree at the University of Bristol but had chosen to stay on in the States at the end of his exchange and had never returned – even to complete his degree.

He had had some interesting experiences over the years, including being a roadie in the music industry, where he had toured with the likes of the Osmonds, Earth, Wind & Fire and Janis Joplin.

He had then become involved in marketing some early computer games, and his experience in software marketing led to his joining Microsoft in 1980, as employee 31 of the company.

He had been given responsibility for the many third-party products that Microsoft sold under their own label in their early years such as the Fortran and Pascal compilers. His star product was Flight Simulator, an airline pilot simulation game developed by Bruce Artwick, who had been persuaded by Boyd to market it under the Microsoft label to huge success.

After Comdex finished, I flew up to visit Microsoft in Bellevue, a suburb of Seattle in Washington State on the Pacific Northwest of the USA. Today, the largest companies in the world are all digital economy companies (such as Microsoft, Apple and Google), but back then the PC industry was young and immature, and although Microsoft in 1983 had a very high profile in what, at the time, was a relatively small PC industry, it wasn't yet a particularly large company. In fact, the entire business was based in a single three-storey building next to Lake Washington.

I met with Boyd to demonstrate our Expert-Ease program to him. He seemed impressed and immediately arranged that I show it to his boss, Bill Gates. At that time Gates was a slim, geeky-looking 28-year-old kid who wore large-framed spectacles. His office was right in the centre of the middle floor of the building, so we popped along and I demonstrated Expert-Ease to him.

He was intrigued. I don't think he had seen anything like it before, but his conclusion was fascinating. He rocked back and forwards in his chair and then declared, "Yep, you can probably sell fifteen hundred of those."

What I didn't then understand, but figured out later, was that he meant that it was the kind of product that would only be bought by 'early adopters', and that there were about 1,500 of these individuals. In the end we did sell around 1,500 copies of Expert-Ease. Not for the first (or last) time, Bill Gates was a superb judge of the market.

Before I left the Microsoft building, Boyd took me to a locked secure room to show me a top-secret new computer from Apple. It was a Macintosh, due to be launched a few months later. Microsoft had been allocated some early computers so that they could develop applications which Apple didn't already have covered, in particular the Microsoft spreadsheet package, Multiplan.

This Macintosh had clearly impressed Gates so much that he had decided to accelerate his own rival development environment, the one that he had referred to at his Comdex opening address, Microsoft Windows, which eventually was launched in a fairly primitive form in November 1985.

I was very impressed with the Macintosh, but not at all surprised. This was the machine that had been strongly rumoured, and that I had been waiting for – a competitively priced personal computer with a powerful graphical user interface, built-in networking and a computer mouse for positioning a pointer on the screen.

It was launched the following January with a blockbuster

advertisement on a 'Big Brother' theme directed by the award-winning movie director Ridley Scott, first aired during the 1984 Super Bowl championship.

ESI was a small company and didn't need a full-time finance person, so we hired a part-timer who popped into the business a couple of days a month to keep the books. He was a tall, thin, weedy, middle-aged individual with thinning hair and a grey moustache but his tastes seemed to be more exotic than his appearance – he drove a fancy sports car, hung out with an attractive younger girlfriend and carried a crocodile-skin briefcase.

These clues should have been warning signs.

One day we became suspicious that the amount of money in our bank account was not as it should be and discovered to our horror that he had been stealing from the company. His method was not particularly sophisticated – he had opened his own bank accounts under the same surname and initials as many of our suppliers and regular contractors and then made out unauthorised payments to them, forging the Director's signature from a previous cheque.

As a result, when anyone saw the payments being made, they recognised the names, and they didn't arouse immediate suspicion. Needless to say, when we discovered the fraud, he quickly disappeared never to be seen again, after having made off with around £15,000, a lot of money in these days for a small start-up company.

This was a good lesson for me – always have a healthy level of suspicion about whether people are behaving properly, keep a rough estimate in your head of the basic finances of your business, watch out for any expenses that suddenly seem unusual, and for any individuals who seem to be spending more than they earn.

In my time at ESI I had been the Technical Director and often deputised for the CEO of the business. I had participated in most of the high-level meetings that we held with various other parties. One day I was in a meeting in central London when our backer Sy Joffe beckoned me over to join him at the window. In the street below was a classic Rolls-Royce car and Sy told me that he had just arranged to buy it. A few months later, when we visited him at his home at Great Neck on Long Island, he insisted that Sandy and I get into the back of this Rolls-Royce while he played the role of chauffeur to drive us to the local shops.

I also joined meetings with various potential sources of fresh investment in the ESI business. At one of these we met with Peter Englander of Alan Patricoff Associates, a venture capital business based at that time in New York and London. Englander was clearly intrigued when he heard about my background in graphics workstation development and showed much more interest in that than he did in ESI. This intrigued me and I began to realise that it might just be possible to raise funding for a start-up business to develop workstation software.

On 4 July 1983, US Independence Day, Sandy Blackie and I were at Sy Joffe's vacation home in Montauk, the beachfront town at the top of Long Island where the seriously rich of New York have their seaside holiday homes. It was a beautiful hot summer's day, and we popped over to the local fish market and bought a few lobsters which we then roasted on a barbeque. They were delicious.

Sandy had just received some very interesting information from his contacts at the Scottish Development Agency back in Glasgow. ICL had been in touch to inform the SDA that they had decided to close their development centre at Dalkeith Palace and would be announcing the closure in a few weeks' time.

This changed everything.

I quickly realised that some of the most talented software engineers I knew would soon become available; and not only that, but these engineers were highly experienced in graphics workstation development, the very skills that had got Peter Englander, the top venture capitalist, intrigued.

I decided there and then that I would try and start a new company.

Sandy was supportive of my plans. I'd never had a major equity stake in ESI and he could see the exciting opportunity that had emerged. Also, he was sure that the closure of Dalkeith would mean that he could also hire talented managers to drive ESI forward. I agreed to stay with ESI until the following May to ensure a smooth handover while taking the time out I needed to start up our own company.

Unfortunately ESI didn't survive for much longer. When I finally left in May 1984 they had 11 employees, but the business failed three months later, by which time they had 24 employees. They appeared to have overextended themselves; when a key new investor pulled out at the last minute there was no alternative plan, and they quickly ran out of money.

5

OWL TAKES WING

As soon as I returned from the trip where I'd learned of the imminent closure of ICL Dalkeith, I called up two key colleagues who were still working there, Stuart Harper and Richard Stonehouse, and invited them round to my house for a chat. Stuart and Richard had headed up the two main development teams on the PERQ project.

Stuart Harper had been a very effective project manager at ICL. Originally hailing from Sheffield, he had shown a strong ability to deliver high-quality development projects. Richard Stonehouse was a studious individual, a mild-mannered bachelor who was a mathematics graduate from the University of Cambridge and had shown that he was capable of some very high-level and precise systems design work. He hailed from Derbyshire in the English Midlands (and had acquired the nickname - 'Sage Derby').

I told them the news about the impending closure of Dalkeith. They didn't believe me at first but were willing to speculate on what might be possible if it turned out to be true. I mentioned that I had met with a venture capitalist who had shown serious interest in our workstations experience, and that

I had also had initial chats with the SDA, who had been supportive. We spoke of others with the appropriate skills that we might attract to start up a business.

Dave McLaren was a highly competent software developer who had turned his hand to a variety of different software projects and had always delivered. I had worked with Dave in the past and would be very happy to have him on the team. Their other suggestion was Gordon Dougan, a quiet, thoughtful and very thorough developer and system designer whom they rated as one of the best. I had never worked with Gordon before but I was happy to accept their judgement.

We had to think of a name for the company. Richard suggested Office Workstations Limited which we could shorten to OWL. The objective was to create business or 'office' software for the emerging personal 'workstations' as they became the standard for business use. We would aim to have our new software on the market as people began to adopt this new type of computer, which we were convinced would soon become available as the next generation of personal computers began to arrive.

So we had the beginning of a team to form our new company, OWL. I would be Chief Executive Officer (CEO), leading the business and driving strategy and business development, Stuart would be Chief Operating Officer (COO) and would be my deputy, taking responsibility for all development activities and operations, as well as keeping track of our initial financial affairs until we could afford a qualified head of finance. Richard would lead on the design specifications for our proposed product, but his precision and attention to detail also made him ideal to take on the role of Company Secretary and supervise our early legal activities. Dave and Gordon would build and lead development teams.

We were then enormously helped by the actions of ICL. As far as ICL management was concerned, it would be very easy to exit from Dalkeith Palace; it would be closed down in September 1983 and, they had assumed, a large proportion of the skilled staff would then transfer to a high-quality new office suite at their Kidsgrove site in Staffordshire to set up the state-of-the-art 'PERQ Development Centre'.

A key element that they hadn't fully thought through is that under UK employment law, it stipulates that anybody being relocated to another part of the country had to be also offered the alternative of taking a redundancy payment instead, and in the case of most of the long-standing Dalkeith employees this payment amounted to around £25,000 each – a decent sum in the early 1980s.

The staff at Dalkeith were addressed at an all-staff meeting by senior ICL management. They were told that ICL had created what they described as 'palatial' accommodation for them at Kidsgrove and that the exciting work that they had been doing on PERQ development would continue there. The plan was to establish a new development group of around 80 staff, and management anticipated that 60% of them would relocate from Dalkeith.

For almost all the experienced software engineers this turned out to be an offer they could easily refuse. ICL was proposing to relocate them from what was, after all, literally a palace, on the outskirts of Edinburgh, one of the most attractive and dynamic cities in Europe, to an office block on the outskirts of Stoke-on-Trent, which really isn't. And if they didn't want to accept the deal the more experienced engineers would get £25,000 cash.

Not surprisingly, almost all took the money. Fewer than 10 agreed to relocate, and they were all relatively junior staff who hadn't yet earned much in the way of redundancy entitlement, or indeed gained much systems development experience. Even Richard Stonehouse, who had been brought up a few miles away from Kidsgrove, didn't give it a second thought.

Now that the closure had been announced, it emerged that I wasn't the only one planning a new company. My successor in charge of the PERQ project, Peter Palmer, was also proposing a new start-up company, and he had assembled his team of five: as well as himself he had signed up Nick Felisiak, John Martin, Andy Davis and Martin Ritchie.

These were all impressive guys but I was particularly disappointed that Martin Ritchie was among them. Despite his surname, Martin was no relation to me, but I had been responsible for persuading him to relocate from the sales and marketing department of ICL to the Dalkeith development office. I was conscious that our team were a bit weak in sales and marketing skills and had he not joined the rival project I would have certainly tried to persuade him to join us. None of my team had any sales or marketing experience and I was aware that if we wanted to build a profitable business, we would have to work out how to develop a commercially successful company.

Peter's new company decided to specialise in another leading-edge innovation which was installed on every PERQ – ethernet networking technology. They developed terminal servers, routers, bridges, analysers and protocol software stacks for various operating systems. Among others, they developed the TCP/IP stack which was licensed to Microsoft to be incorporated into Microsoft Windows, enabling those PCs to be networked. They called their networking technology company Spider Systems. When we bumped into each other from time to time and gentle ribbing ensued, I wasn't always able to resist the temptation to point out that owls were known to eat spiders.

Spider turned out also to be a successful business and was finally acquired by Shiva Corporation in 1995.

∽

IN 1987, Peter Palmer and I met up in a pub one lunchtime and we concluded that what Scotland needed was a trade body for the software industry. With some help from the SDA we managed to set up a new organisation to represent our industry, which we called the Scottish Software House Federation (SSHF). When we set it up, we had to determine a few rules for companies qualifying to be members so that it would be seen that the organisation represented serious businesses as opposed to one-man bands. We decided that companies eligible to join should be at least three years old and have a turnover of at least £500,000. It was after we had set these admission criteria that we realised that our own two companies didn't yet quite qualify under these criteria. Of course, it was just a few months before we did and Peter became the first Chairman of SSHF and I took over as the second.

In subsequent years the SSHF has gone on to become Scot-landIS, one of the largest trade associations in the country representing an industry of over 2,000 companies employing over 70,000 individuals and annual revenues in excess of £4 billion, in total about 3% of the Scottish economy.

ONCE ICL HAD ANNOUNCED the closure of Dalkeith, we were then free to start planning our new company, which unlike Spider was to be software-based. We knew we had to exploit our PERQ experience, and we were also convinced that future low-cost personal computers would, like the Apple Macintosh, use a graphics display and a computer mouse.

We considered what kind of applications would be most suitable for these new computing environments and we concluded that databases or spreadsheets were relatively usable on current text-based displays, but that when creating documents, it would be a significant advantage to have a graphics display. Documents could then resemble, on the screen, as closely as possible the final document on the page, using a variety of typefaces and incorporating layout, graphics and images.

We decided that we would create a heavyweight document creation system – one that would be ideal for professional document authors to use to set standards for layout, typography etc, and which would automatically look after document structures such as section numbering, contents lists, indexing, reference linking and so on. It would manage multi-volume documents and be ideal for everything from small documents to large sets of technical manuals.

Richard started leading the team in defining this major product and a great deal of work went into getting it right. It became the basis of the business plan which was to be presented to raise venture capital. We were going to develop and market a blockbuster comprehensive document management product. I was still working at ESI but Tommy Thomas agreed to lend us an empty office in early December 1983 at Edinburgh University's High Performance Computer Centre at the rural Bush estate, around 8 miles south of the city, where the university also based much of its agricultural veterinary function.

We started trading, firstly as a partnership, and when ICL found that very few of their skilled developers had agreed to move to their new Kidsgrove development centre, they asked us to undertake several key projects on the PERQ under subcontract for them. This was an unexpected source of commercial business that allowed us to book very welcome revenue in our early months of trading.

Meanwhile I started trying to figure out how to start a company from scratch and got a lot of help from the SDA. They referred me to their investment division, Scottish Development Finance (SDF), and I started discussions with one of their executives there, a very helpful Geoff Burns. Although SDF were fully commercial in their investment criteria, they were much friendlier than full-blooded venture capitalists and we were able to rehearse our pitch on them, take advice and improve on it before we delivered it to real hard-nosed venture capitalist companies.

SDF had investment policies that were constrained by European Union state aid rules; they were not able to lead an investment, but they could match the terms of a commercial investment as long as they did so on exactly the same basis as the other, commercial, investors. They were also limited to owning no more than 30% of any company's equity. So we needed at least one 'real' venture capital investor to lead and match the SDF investment, and the one that quickly emerged was Investors in Industry, known as 3i.

This firm dated its existence back to the end of the Second World War, when the UK government strong-armed the major UK banks to set up a risk-capital investment subsidiary, under the threat of potential nationalisation if they refused to do so. Thus, the Industrial and Commercial Finance Corporation (ICFC), as it was initially called, was formed with all the major banks as shareholders. Over the following years it had opened investment offices throughout the UK and in 1983 had renamed itself Investors in Industry, shortened to 3i.

(Later, in 1987, the business was privatised when the various banks sold off their shares, and in 1994 it was floated as a public company on the London Stock Exchange. Gradually, 3i moved away from venture capital investments towards private equity activities, and they closed most of their UK offices).

But back in 1984, 3i had investment offices in Edinburgh and Glasgow and I started discussions with Jim Martin, who headed up their Edinburgh office and seemed fairly enthusiastic about our proposed new company. We had a due diligence visit from their Solihull-based technical specialists and we also got a positive report from them.

Between us all we drafted the outline of an investment proposal. We, the five founders, would put £50,000 into the business and we proposed to raise £250,000 of external venture capital for a total start up investment of £300,000. Our willingness to put 'skin in the game' to the tune of £50,000 was very well received by the investors as it demonstrated a real commitment to the company. The outside investors would own 62.5% of the company and we would retain 37.5% between us.

Meanwhile, I asked my contacts at the SDA who they would recommend as advisors to the business. They gave me three names: Bryan Rankin of accountants Thomson McLintock, John Rafferty of lawyers WJ Burness WS and Gavin Masterton at the Bank of Scotland. (Thomson McLintock later became part of the international accountancy firm KPMG, and WJ Burness are now known as Burness Paull LLP.)

I followed up on all three of these and they were all happy to take us on. These were excellent introductions; it turned out that they were three of the most senior executives in Edinburgh's commercial scene, at that time largely centred around the city's Charlotte Square financial district. Rafferty and Rankin were the senior partners of their relative businesses and Masterton was responsible for all the east of Scotland operations of the Bank of Scotland.

The Bank of Scotland was originally established in 1695, and by the mid-1980s had established a reputation as one of the best-managed banks in the UK, although in those days it was mostly a regional bank which concentrated on serving the banking needs of the Scottish economy.

We met with Masterton at his office in the imposing Bank of Scotland headquarters at the top of the Mound, facing across to Princes Street in the very heart of Edinburgh. He had only just returned from a three-month intensive executive development course at Harvard University and was clearly fired up by his exposure to the dynamic business scene in Boston, one of the world's leading technology and innovation centres.

Masterton recommended a bank manager, David Gibson, at their headquarters branch and we opened our business account with him. We had a variety of bank managers over the years that followed, but I was always conscious that Masterton remained a key supporter behind the scenes, particularly when we later sought substantial bank loans to support the business.

We really needed one more investor and I reconnected with Peter Englander at Alan Patricoff, but he seemed to have cooled off on the opportunity. I also had several meetings with David Quysner at London-based Abingworth but in the end he also didn't want to proceed. The London investment community at that time seemed to be rather preoccupied with the emerging new technology of cellular radio, which promised to create what later turned out to be the massive mobile phone industry.

Although they all seemed convinced about the prospects for mobile telephony, they were notably more sceptical about the development of personal computers. When I said that everybody would soon have their own personal computer, they mostly demurred: 'No, I don't think so. My secretary will use the computer in the office' was a typical response.

Things were not going as well as I'd hoped. Although the deal could be done with just 3i and SDF, it would be much better if we had a third investor. Geoff Burns gave me the name and contact details of a long-shot possibility – Doug Fairservice at a company called Candover Investment Ltd – and I arranged a meeting with him.

So, on 1 June 1984 I met with Doug at his office a stone's throw from Fleet Street. Fairservice was a London-based Scot who had previously worked at the British Technology Group (BTG) before joining Candover. BTG was a government agency which in the past had enjoyed the automatic rights to commercially exploit any research emanating from publicly funded UK research, such as any innovation generated by our leading universities, so he was very familiar with commercialising advanced technology.

I met with Doug at 9.30 and we hit it off immediately. By 11am he had agreed to invest along with 3i and SDF and to join our board as a Non-Executive Director.

Looking back, I never ever worked out why he did this. Candover was a mature investment company which normally invested £2m or more in companies. It also had a stated policy of never investing in pre-revenue and computing companies. Even though we seemed to break all their investment rules, he was willing to take a piece of our tiny £250,000 deal.

The deal was then pulled together very quickly. We were already spending the original £50,000 that we had put up in operating the business and our investors proposed that they would invest in stages. They would put up an initial tranche of £125,000 and if all went well after our first year, they agreed to invest the second tranche of £125,000. Three-quarters of our cash injection, £37,500, would be used to buy real ordinary shares and the remaining £12,500 was to buy deferred convertible shares, which would convert one-for-one into real shares at the second tranche. Thus, we would not be further diluted when the planned second tranche was invested later.

Of course, it also gave the investors the added option of pulling out after our first year if we didn't deliver a decent initial year's performance.

Our money was to be used to buy ordinary shares, but the investors insisted on special CCPPO shares – 'cumulative, convertible, participating, preferred-dividend, ordinary'. Despite the final word, these were far from being ordinary; it gave them various rights to future profit-sharing dividends. If we didn't manage to eventually provide an exit for the investors, these dividends would become due and would increasingly bear down on us.

The message was clear – we were expected to build a business and either sell it or list it on a stock market so that the investors would get a substantial gain on their investment. That was the goal.

The company would create 100,000 shares – 62,500 CCPPOs for the investors against our initial 37,500 ordinary shares – but we also retained our 12,500 convertible shares for the next tranche.

We had already discussed the composition of our board. I would serve as CEO, and Stuart Harper and Richard Stonehouse would join me as Executive Board Directors. Both SDF and 3i did not want to appoint company directors but retained monitoring rights and were able to attend board meetings at any time. Doug Fairservice of Candover had already agreed to become a Non-Executive Director but we still needed to find a Non-Executive Chairman. It was suggested that the ideal candidate might be a current or recently retired senior manager in an internationally minded, preferably technology-based, Scottish company. One candidate I spoke with had recently retired from running John Menzies, the distributor and high-street retailer of newspapers and magazines, but I didn't really think he had enough experience of the high-tech world for our needs.

The other candidate who was suggested was Graham Bowen, who was then Chief Executive of a Fife-based technology company called Compugraphics. Compugraphics was Europe's leading manufacturer of high-quality photomasks, which were used by silicon chip manufacturers to enable their wafer lithography processes to create complex processor chips. We decided that he was sufficiently high-tech and internationally minded and agreed that he be appointed non-executive Chairman.

Our board was complete.

At an early meeting, Graham Bowen suggested to me that it was appropriate that I should have a slightly larger equity stake than my fellow founders as I was to carry the leadership role. So we decided that I would put up £12,000 and the other four would put £9,500 each, making up our total of £50,000.

The investment agreement turned out to be a mammoth tome. It was led by 3i and seemed to me to be an exercise in legal archaeology – it looked like every time that 3i had had any problem with a previous investee company, a new clause was drafted to be inserted into their standard investment agreement which tried to avoid such a circumstance ever happening again. The resulting investment documentation was over 80 pages long.

In any case we were in fact nearly done. The investors appointed Maclay Murray and Spens LLP, another top firm of Edinburgh lawyers on the opposite corner of Charlotte Square. The deal was completed and £125,000 was paid into our bank account.

Office Workstations Limited was born on 1 July 1984. We were a real company at last.

6

GETTING STARTED

We had our borrowed office out at the Bush estate but that was always a temporary solution. Now that we had our funding secured, we needed a permanent office. We also needed somebody to sort out our activities, help us find proper accommodation and handle all our admin hassle.

We needed an administrator.

We quickly decided that our first hire should be Carol Brown, who had been both the most efficient and one of the least flappable of the office workers team at ICL Dalkeith. Her last job there was assistant to the Human Resources Manager and she had also started the process of getting some HR qualifications herself, so she was capable of supervising our hiring and employee contracting processes.

Stuart and I called on her at her house. She had got a job shelf-stacking at a supermarket, and she said that she was quite happy doing that 'thanks very much'.

We left, disappointed.

We went back a few days later to have another go. We told her we couldn't understand how she could possibly prefer a dead-end job in a supermarket to joining us in an ambitious exciting new company that was going to take on the world. She was somehow convinced by the argument this time and agreed to join us.

Edinburgh Council had repurposed a Victorian primary school at the top of Easter Road, which they had optimistically named Abbeymount Techbase. It was quite similar to the primary school in New Street that had been the base for ESI and, like that one, was a relatively cheap and flexible space. Offices in Edinburgh City Centre were at a premium, expensive, and in those days typically involved taking on a long lease. That obviously didn't suit a high-tech company like us – we had no idea how big we would be in three years' time, far less in a decade's time. The Council, however, was offering flexible accommodation in their Victorian school building, which only needed a few weeks' notice to quit.

Although the Council had repurposed the old school, this amounted to little more than hanging a sign outside and clearing the old classrooms. I asked a friend who had refurbished a couple of rental properties and knew a few tradesmen if he would help us make it office ready. The classrooms had very high ceilings and so we dropped large paper globe lights, creating a false-ceiling effect. My wife Barbara, still a tax inspector, had heard that the Inland Revenue were replacing old desks and chairs in one of their Edinburgh offices with new office furniture.

We bought the lot.

The desks were pretty sturdy and didn't need much renovation but the office chairs looked a bit tired, so Barbara and I refurbished them with new material and a staple gun. We were still very much in start-up mode – we weren't about to spend any money if it could possibly be avoided.

We had also bought several Apple Macintoshes, the computer that most resembled the computing environment that we needed, but at a personal computer price. Even so, these cost about £2,000 each, at 1984 prices. It is interesting to note that today's massively more powerful computers are now much cheaper.

Richard was busy specifying his comprehensive large-scale document management system, but Gordon and Dave were mostly still working on projects for ICL. We remained very happy to take on development projects for ICL – at a good price. It even allowed us to hire more ex-Dalkeith staff to deliver this work.

Another opportunity that we progressed was to apply to become part of the UK government's Alvey Programme. After Sir James Lighthill's report in 1971, most UK AI research had gone unfunded and much had withered away, but in 1981 the Japanese government announced an ambitious 'fifth generation' project to boost their advanced computer research activities, and this had caused a degree of panic among all levels of the UK's computing community, all the way up to the Minister for Information Technology in the UK Government, a charismatic and enthusiastic politician called Kenneth Baker.

Baker commissioned Sir John Alvey to study how the UK, which had always held a strong position in computing research, could respond to the Japanese challenge and Alvey recommended a special programme to fund consortiums of academics and industrialists in partnerships to jointly develop breakthrough computing technologies.

The Alvey Programme had five major components: VLSI (very large-scale integration) technology for microelectronics; Intelligent Knowledge Based Systems (IKBS) or Artificial Intelligence; Software Engineering; Man–Machine Interface (included natural language processing); and Systems Architecture (for parallel processing).

We were sure we fitted in there somewhere – we were certainly working on some innovative software for new graphics-based computing environments and we were planning to develop new highly effective man-machine interfaces.

It was suggested we should consider joining an emerging consortium which was to be led by the engineering company GEC to work on novel publishing technology. Stuart Harper and I set off to meet up with the main proposed participants of this consortium on 12th and 13th June 1984. We drove down to the London area and met with the existing consortium partners: Monotype, GEC and the IAPRC, a research centre for the printing and publishing industry. As a result of these discussions, we agreed in principle to join this Alvey project which was concerned with advanced publishing technologies.

The British Computer Society (BCS) is the UK-based professional institution for computing; it operates via local branches and at that time I served on the committee of the Edinburgh branch (much later, in the late 1990s, I was to be elected BCS President) – but it also operated a set of specialist groups in various fields of computing. One of these was the BCS Electronic Publishing Specialist Group (EPSG). While we were down south, we'd also arranged to meet up on the Wednesday afternoon with the Chair of the BCS EPSG, Heather Brown, a senior lecturer in computing at the University of Kent at Canterbury, so we drove over to Canterbury to meet up with her.

We asked Heather for guidance about any relevant innovative research activity into electronic publishing that was already underway in the UK so that we might seek to build a relationship with them. She wasn't very hopeful; there wasn't much of interest going on in the UK, she said, but there were several interesting companies that she knew of in the USA. She gave us some contacts there, including at Adobe and Aldus.

"While you're here anyway," she said, "you might want to have a word with my husband, Professor Peter Brown, who has

been working on some interesting ideas for reading documentation from a screen."

She phoned Peter. It was around 3.45 and he was due to give
a lecture at 4pm but he agreed to give us a quick 10 minutes or
so. When we popped down to his office, he explained the issue
that he had set out to solve. "When people are using the PERQ
and need to look up a technical detail," he said, 'they invariably
pull a bound volume of a printed technical manual off the shelf
despite the fact that the full user and technical manual is
online on the computer – but nobody ever uses the online
version.'

His conclusion was that it was too difficult to navigate an
online manual and much easier to find your way around a
printed volume. In looking for a solution to this problem he set
about developing a new method of displaying documentation
on a screen that was easier to navigate.

He called his system 'Guide'.

He used the computer mouse on the PERQ to point to
'hotspots' on the screen. When he clicked the mouse, the
hotspot would open out, displaying content that had been
hidden underneath, and this process could be repeated again
and again, expanding each time.

The effect of this was that a document could be entirely
shown initially as just its contents page, but with a couple of
clicks, sections and subsections could be quickly opened out;
another click and they could be folded back away again.

He had one more trick. Some of the hotspots were desig-
nated as 'note' hotspots and when clicked on, a small piece of
text, like a Post-it note, would pop up on the screen showing
added information. This was the equivalent of a reference or a
footnote in a document.

Stuart and I were very intrigued by this fascinating system
and asked him if he had any information about it. He pulled a

slim technical paper off the pile of documents on his desk, wrote '£10' at the top of the front page, and handed it over.

We never did pay him that £10, although later we did find other ways of rewarding Peter.

On our way back to Edinburgh, Stuart and I discussed what we had seen on our two-day trip. The Alvey consortium didn't look particularly exciting but just might be a suitable way to support some of our R&D and, if it took us into real documentation applications, might be of value.

We had been much more interested in Peter Brown's 'dynamic documentation' system, as he had called it. We decided that we might just follow up on that.

The next month, July 1984, I made a visit to the USA to follow up on some of Heather Brown's contacts. In silicon valley I visited Chuck Geschke at Adobe, which had been a spin-out from Xerox PARC and was known to be developing the PostScript type-definition language based on concepts they had worked on at PARC. They had also started to licence many proprietary typefaces from foundries such as Linotype and ITC. Clearly a PostScript-based laser printer, when it became available, would be a revolutionary product for the future of publishing, enabling almost anybody to create complex documents using a variety of fonts and images.

Adobe had yet to install their technology on any actual printer and Geschke told me that he was unable to disclose who they were working with but that it was a company which 'shipped a lot of 68000-based computers'. And just in case I had been too dumb to realise who he meant (which I hadn't) there was a solitary business card sitting on his desk with an Apple logo on it.

I also went to visit VisiCorp. VisiCorp was the Silicon Valley company which had marketed the original VisiCalc from the Boston-based developers, Software Arts. However, with the arrival of the IBM PC and the Lotus 1-2-3 spreadsheet, VisiCalc was losing its leadership position and VisiCorp had decided that they would develop their own new proprietary windowing system, called VisiOn, along with a whole range of applications, all of which were intended to run on standard IBM-compatible personal computers.

I called on Digital Research, the company that had originally misjudged the opportunity with IBM to supply the PC operating system, but who were now working, like VisiCorp, on a set of new applications, including a sophisticated document management package.

I also went to see MicroPro, the developers of the then leading word processing package, WordStar and they also seemed to have ambitious plans for enhanced versions of their word processor systems.

Finally, I went up to Seattle and visited Aldus. I didn't meet their CEO Paul Brainerd on that trip, but I met with a senior lieutenant in his company who demonstrated an early version of PageMaker.

I returned from the States suitably chastened about the prospects of our innovative comprehensive document management package. It seemed to me that there were several west coast US companies who were both very well-funded and already way ahead of us. When these products did get released, they would be backed by the marketing muscle of companies with substantial resources behind them.

Who were we kidding, thinking that we could make an impact in such a crowded market when so far all we had raised was a measly £175,000?

We decided to actively follow up with Peter Brown's intriguing technology as an alternative strategy. It was genuinely innovative, and I wasn't aware of anybody anywhere who was working on anything similar. Also, it seemed to us that, as computer displays improved, more and more people would prefer to read documents off a screen. Although the original Macintosh displayed at only 72 dpi resolution it could display different fonts and layouts – but we had been familiar with the PERQ's high resolution 300 dpi display. Surely it was only a matter of time before other displays would also be improved?

We decided that we would put our best software architect, Gordon Dougan, on the job. We arranged to get a copy of Peter Brown's Guide for the PERQ sent up and Gordon set about creating a product for the Apple Macintosh (Mac) based on Peter's original concepts. Gordon set about this task with his normal thoroughness and within a few months he had a working demonstrator system.

I was still worried that we needed to get some marketing skills into the company, and I arranged to have dinner near Windsor with Roger Vinniecombe, who had headed up the marketing of the PERQ at ICL. He was unconvinced that joining us was a good move for him at that time, as he was still involved at ICL enthusiastically trying to sell PERQ systems. Later, he and Reg Chamberlain left ICL to form Advent Systems, to market the Accent Unix system.

Our first year was a successful one, but not exactly in the way we had predicted. We continued to benefit from ICL's requirement to access our experienced PERQ engineering skills and, after the demise of ESI, we were also able to build on our specialist knowledge of the ID3 expert system induction algorithm – which was technology in the public domain– and our copy protection technology, originally developed by David Corner, which we now called Protector.

As we grew, we were able to hire more key staff, including Phil Cooke and Robbie McLaren. Phil had been doing a Physics PhD at Jodrell Bank before joining ICL, where he had very quickly established himself as a superb systems architect. We had wanted Phil to be one of our founding team but as he was a relatively recent hire at ICL, his redundancy payment wasn't large, and he was forced to get a better-paid job elsewhere in the meantime. As soon as we could guarantee steady employment, we hired Phil, and he later became the key figure leading our solutions business.

Robbie McLaren had an interesting background. His father had been a Scottish soldier who had met and married Robbie's Japanese mother while posted to post-war Japan. Taking after his mother, Robbie had a distinctive Japanese appearance. Unfortunately, the only language he could actually speak was a Scottish-accented version of English – the ability to speak and understand Japanese would have turned out later to be a huge advantage. Robbie took on the role of Product Marketing Manager of the Guide product, pulling together the feature set, documentation and so on.

We also decided to hire David Corner, for obvious reasons, Brian Newton, a very talented developer, and Lynda Hardman, a Maths graduate from Glasgow who had also worked at ICL and who went on to project manage the development of Guide.

Gordon Dougan was making good progress on the Macintosh Guide. In the event, he was never able to use any of the code from the original Pascal-based University of Kent version, as the Macintosh development environment was so different. He did, however, create one key new user interface innovation.

Peter Brown's original system had developed buttons which enabled a replacement 'stretch-text' effect and pop-up notes, but because Peter was a good classic computer scientist, he believed in structured program design and had adopted the philosophy outlined in Edsger Dijkstra's famous letter 'GoTo Statement Considered Harmful' (in the March 1968 edition of the 'Communications of the ACM' journal), in which he criticised the use of the GoTo statement in programming languages of the day.

Dijkstra had maintained that a 'GoTo' in a programme

leads to a natural complexity that can make the logic of a programme difficult to follow. He proposed an alternative structure which involved calling various subroutines embedded within programmes.

As a result, Peter hadn't included a button which enabled you to simply jump from one part to another part of a document, or indeed to a completely different document.

We discovered that not having such a mechanism didn't really work in practice. To usefully navigate complex documentation, especially multi-section or multi-volume ones, you needed a GoTo – a pointer that took you from one place in the documentation set directly to another point. This turned out to be the key feature of our system – this was the 'hypertext link' – the fundamental technique that underpins the hypertext model (although at that time we were still unaware that the technology we were developing already had a name).

Of course, this model can also create the unstructured nature of documentation collections leading to what became known as the 'lost in hypertext' problem.

Meanwhile, I had been negotiating with the commercialisation team at the University of Kent. They had started quite heavy, demanding 20% royalties on sales of our product and each of us placing severe restrictions on what the other party was allowed to do. Our respective lawyers were running up lots of billable time arguing with each other, but we didn't seem to be getting anywhere.

Eventually I decided to call a halt to this, and I sat down with Peter Brown, who I knew to be a very reasonable person. We agreed that we would provide an immediate lump sum to the university in full payment for the original concept, which they would split between Peter Brown, his team and the university. We wouldn't actively market his PERQ version of the software but if we did find a customer for it, we agreed we would pay them a substantial royalty. They were also free to both sell their version and to continue unrestricted their research activities into their dynamic documentation innovations.

This was a good deal for both of us. With the considerable help of the international profile gained by our publishing Guide, Professor Brown went on to be recognised internationally as a leading figure in hypertext research, building a successful research team in what was fast becoming a topical new research area.

We also agreed to employ Peter as a technical consultant and advisor to OWL for 10 days per year at a rate of £500 per day (and guaranteed him the £5,000 whether we used this time or not). Our product, which although inspired by his original concepts had never used any of his code, and which by now had diverged substantially from the original, particularly with our inclusion of the hypertext link, would completely belong to us and we would be unfettered in exploiting it.

That was all agreed. It was an early lesson in handling university commercialisation teams and how not to let the lawyers get control of the process. Be clear about what you want to achieve and try to give the other side what they want to achieve – in this case what they mostly wanted was unfettered rights to continue their own research.

Then tell the lawyers and the university to make it happen.

I CONTINUED to visit the USA and made a point of meeting with anybody who could be useful to us. I knew that Guide was genuinely innovative, and I felt sure that there was a US corporation somewhere that would be keen to market it for us. I had taken note of how Boston's Software Arts had published VisiCalc through the Silicon Valley-based corporation that became VisiCorp.

One individual who was extremely helpful to us turned out

to be Carl Bascombe, who was employed by the UK trade office part of the UK consulate in San Francisco. He was a well-connected American whose job it was to help British technology business with introductions to key individuals in the Silicon Valley tech scene. He seemed to know everybody who was important in the personal computer software industry, and he gave me lots of very senior contacts.

By this time, we had an early prototype of Guide. It was time to show it to a few industry leaders and get their reaction.

Robbie McLaren came along with me in March 1985 on a trip which took in Seattle, Los Angeles, San Francisco and New York. By this time, we had developed a corporate policy that it was best, if at all possible, to do such trips with at least two people. It is surprising how a single individual can misread a meeting or miss an important point. Discussing meetings after they were finished often revealed something that one or the other had missed. It was more expensive, of course, but we still thought it worth it.

In Seattle I reacquainted myself with Alan Boyd, who I had dealt with over the *Expert-Ease* product. Alan was the executive at Microsoft responsible for third party-acquired products sold under the Microsoft brand and they were my preferred choice to market Guide.

The pattern turned out to be like my previous visit. We demonstrated Guide to him, and he was clearly impressed by it – this was completely different from anything he had seen before. A quick phone call and we were once more over in Bill Gates's office showing it to him. He was also impressed. We agreed to keep them informed as we developed our program towards a shippable product.

We had bought a cheap ticket to fly with TWA from Seattle to San Francisco. What we had failed to realise was that this involved flying to and from their US hub which was based in St Louis – this was the equivalent of flying from London to Edinburgh via Athens. What should have been a two-hour flight turned out to be ten hours long.

After we had bought our ticket to San Francisco, we later arranged to meet up with some ex-ICL friends who were now working in Los Angeles. There was nothing for it but to drive the six hours or so to LA in our unlimited mileage hire car. It turned out to be quite a long day.

After an enjoyable weekend break in Los Angeles we set off to drive back up to Silicon Valley to visit Apple Computer in Cupertino. As we entered the reception area at Apple, Steve Jobs rushed out, barking orders over his shoulder at his trailing assistant. All of this bumping into industry legends had a bit of an effect on Robbie McLaren – having been in the presence of both Bill Gates and Steve Jobs within a few days, it seemed to me that his brain was beginning to overload.

Our appointment was with one of their 'evangelists' – this being literally the job description that they had printed on their business cards – Alain Rossmann, an individual within Apple whose job was to help companies who wanted to market software for release on the Mac.

Although the Mac had been announced in January 1984, there was still quite a shortage of software for this novel type of computer. The IBM PC and its competitors had been around for several years and had lots of software available. By contrast, the new, innovative Macintosh was having difficulty making an impact against the rather more established IBM, and was struggling to meet its targets, particularly in professional applications. For many users IBM sold the professional computer and the graphics-rich Macintosh was often perceived, quite unjustly, as a but of a toy. One year after the launch of the Macintosh, the aging Apple II even represented 85% of Apple's sales.

As a result, Apple were very keen to encourage any company which wanted to launch new software packages, particularly ones which demonstrated the advantages of the Macintosh graphics/mouse environment. They were very impressed with our pilot version of Guide and agreed to help us to find marketing partners.

We also met with Digital Research, who were developing a windowing environment for PCs that they called GEM. We visited Interleaf, who had developed a heavyweight document publishing system similar to our original concept but for expensive 32-bit computers. And we met with Electronic Arts, which was mostly a leading computer games company but also had an interest in other application areas; they wanted to know whether we could develop a 'what you see is what you get' (WYSIWYG) document processing package for some of their markets. Of course we could and we enthusiastically followed up on that project.

We then visited VisiCorp which, on the back of sales of the hugely successful VisiCalc, had now turned into a very large company, and had hired scores of developers building a suite of applications based on their own proprietary windowing system for the PC. We met in a glass-framed office looking over a huge open-plan office containing the sea of developers, all working on what was intended to become a complete advanced window-based environment, complete with all the key applications – databases, spreadsheets and document processors. It had been reported that at one point they had been in discussions to merge with Microsoft but the merger discussions had failed. (It turned out that their new system didn't go on to gain much market traction – the next time we visited VisiCorp, a few years later, the company had mostly collapsed: they were down to two rooms, and the phone was ringing off the hook with people calling, trying to get their bills paid. The company was finally sold in a 'fire sale' to Paladin Software.)

We finally wound up our trip in New York, again visiting various contacts, but when we popped into the computer store in the basement of the McGraw-Hill building on the Avenue of the Americas in central Manhattan we noticed that the new Apple LaserWriter had arrived that very day. The LaserWriter had been announced in January but hadn't shipped in the USA until March and wouldn't be available in other countries for several more months.

The Apple LaserWriter came equipped with Adobe's Post-Script and connected via the built-in AppleTalk networking to groups of Macs. It cost $6,995. We decided to buy one right there on the spot and take it back to Edinburgh that evening on our flight home.

I had my recently acquired American Express card on me, which I had been told didn't have any spending limit, so I tried to buy one of these printers. The salesman was also keen to make the sale, but he couldn't get approval from American Express, their UK Brighton office having closed for the night. It was frustrating, but we couldn't come back the next day to complete the deal as we were booked to fly back to the UK that evening.

As evidenced from our cheap TWA ticket deal, we tried hard not to spend too much money. Robbie complained that we had spent that whole week eating at MacDonald's which I'm sure was a bit of an exaggeration. However, we were always willing to spend money when we needed to, and we didn't give a second thought to finding the seven grand to acquire the first LaserWriter in the UK.

We got in touch with a contact we knew in New York and asked him to purchase an Apple LaserWriter for us and ship it to Edinburgh for a small handling fee. He was happy to do that and within a few days the LaserWriter showed up at our office at the top of Easter Road in Edinburgh. We had the first one anywhere outside the USA.

We decided to invite a couple of local business contacts, Derek and Mike Gray, round to see this LaserWriter in action.

Derek and Mike were two brothers who ran a local business called McQueens. It had started as a family-owned office supplies and printing business in the Scottish Borders, but in recent years they had built a technology systems dealership based in Edinburgh and Glasgow, and along the way had set themselves up as Apple resellers.

McQueens was an ambitious company, later becoming the UK distributor for Aldus PageMaker and advising the marketing team at Apple UK. Derek Gray drove the campaign to promote the adoption of PageMaker throughout Europe, which was so successful that it was subsequently adopted across the whole of Apple worldwide. They also set up a production factory for the manufacture of international versions of PageMaker, after which they won the business of manufacturing European editions of other software products. Later they set up a multilingual contact centre in Edinburgh to provide first-line support across Europe for a variety of international software companies.

After initially successfully handling distribution of Page-Maker throughout Europe, Derek Gray was appointed the European VP for Aldus and played a key role in the acquisition of Aldus by Adobe, finally becoming Adobe's global VP for sales and marketing, while all the time remaining based in Edinburgh.

We developed a strong relationship with Derek Gray which resulted in various joint business opportunities in the coming years. We wrote specialised applications for them, including various 'type effects' packages which could be used by typesetting artists to make innovative variants of typefaces for use in documents, signs, and adverts, and they became the UK distributor for our product, Guide.

In June 1985 I was back in the USA to follow up with Electronic Arts, who were keen on progressing their WYSIWYG document package. I also met with leading database company Ashton-Tate, and then Microsoft.

The meeting with Microsoft this time was with a much more substantial team, including Joe Rehfeld, who looked after Microsoft's Mac products, Laura Kemp, in charge of documentation, and Phil Fawcett, who supervised technology development and told us about their plans for their new Microsoft Windows and offered to sign us up with development kits.

This was getting more serious. Could I dare to hope that Microsoft might really be interested in marketing Guide?

I then spent some time at Aldus, also based in Seattle, and this time I got a substantial demonstration of PageMaker, which was due to be released the following month, July 1985. They showed some interest in Guide but clearly, they had quite enough on their plate with the launch of their flagship product, PageMaker.

PageMaker turned out later to be a great success, both for Aldus and for Apple, as many people worldwide adopted the combination of the Apple Mac, LaserWriter and PageMaker for an innovative new technology collectively known as 'desktop publishing'. For the first time ever there was a relatively low-cost way of easily typesetting, laying out and printing sophisticated documents; it created a market sector that made best use of the features that Apple did best.

Desktop publishing arguably rescued the otherwise struggling Apple Mac computer in the mid-1980s. It was an breakthrough use of a computer, and in particular one which, at that time, could not be done on an IBM PC.

I had arranged to go back to Microsoft to see how Alan Boyd wanted to take things forward and I hung around downtown Seattle waiting for what I judged to be the right moment. I visited a bookshop and coffee bar in Pioneer Square to pass the time and eventually worked up the nerve to phone Alan Boyd using one of the payphones in the

Square (mobile phones still being a device of the distant future).

Boyd seemed happy to hear from me and invited me straight over to Microsoft's building on the east side of Lake Washington. When I arrived, we chatted about how the review meeting had gone with his colleagues for a while and then he said, "Let's pop into my office for a minute."

With the door closed behind him he made his pitch: "How about," he said, "we don't go with Microsoft to publish your product, but instead I leave Microsoft and join you guys? We could set up an office here to package and sell your product."

This, frankly, was not what I had wanted to hear.

I had convinced myself that our skills were in software development and that a major US software publisher would look after our sales and marketing. Quite how, I pondered, could a tiny, underfunded, Scottish company possibly package, market and sell a software product in the USA and across the world?

Boyd explained to me that he had seen a few great opportunities get away over the years as Bill Gates had turned them all down. Mitch Kapor had come along to see if Microsoft were interested in publishing Lotus 1-2-3 but he had been rejected. Later Paul Brainerd had demonstrated PageMaker, which Gates had dismissed as just a fancy word processor.

Boyd thought that with Guide we had something really exciting and that, with him on board we could really make something of it.

This was not a situation I had remotely envisaged, but I have always made a point of being open minded and have always been willing to investigate any new opportunity and at least consider if there is any merit in it.

I recalled that Doug Fairservice, our Non-Executive Director from Candover, happened to be visiting Silicon Valley that week so I called Doug and suggested that Alan and I fly down for a meeting with him. He was happy to meet us the following evening for dinner.

We flew down and met with Doug. He was normally a fairly dour Scotsman, but he was clearly quite intrigued by our ideas. My guess is that our investors had been impressed during our first year with our ability to develop great innovative technology but had also worried about our ability to market our products, particularly in a world where the personal computer software business was substantially based on the west coast of the USA. Here was the chance to hire a highly experienced executive from the largest PC software company in the world complete with all his experience in software packaging and distribution as well as his extensive knowledge of appropriate personal computer trade shows and media, and software sales channels.

I came back to Edinburgh and discussed it with my colleagues. Like me, this was not a development that they had anticipated, but it did sound adventurous and exciting, even if it still seemed somehow implausible. Could we really do it? We had no real idea whether we could, but we thought we'd follow it up. Alan agreed to come over to Edinburgh and we would see if we could make it work.

The upshot of our discussions was that we would set up OWL International Inc. as a wholly owned subsidiary of our UK parent company. Alan Boyd would become President of the US business and also Marketing Director of the parent company, and he would serve on the main UK board. He would use his experience of software publishing to gain us publishing contracts for our software. We were also happy to discover from our friends at the SDA that setting up our US operation would attract a 50% grant from a UK government project called the Market Entry Guarantee Scheme.

There was the trickier matter of Boyd's equity stake in OWL. He was clearly core to the future of the business and he expressed the view that he should end up with a similar equity share to mine. As he was a US resident and taxpayer, we didn't have the kind of tax difficulties that arise with awarding shares and share options to UK residents. We made an extremely generous calculation of all the stuff – computers, printers etc. that he was bringing into the business, and we accepted all that as 'payment' for real shares, amounting to around 3% of the equity. The rest he would receive over the next few years as regular awards of share options.

We had been ready to call down our second tranche of £125,000, which had been agreed with our investors at £1 per share, but this latest development was clearly a game-changer.

We had made sales of £106,000 in our first year, a lot better than the £64,000 we had forecast in our original business plan, and our loss, at £84,000, was much lower than the £133,000 in our plan. We had been very lucky; a lot of this impressive performance had been due to ICL making a mess of its PERQ transfer and having been forced to contract us to complete key projects, along with the demise of ESI, where we had been able to pick up expertise in expert systems and copy protection technology. It was highly unusual for a start-up tech company to do so much better than the plan in its first year, and it indicated that, despite being basically a bunch of development engineers, we could generate revenue.

However, the biggest opportunity was our new business model, which involved hiring one of the key executives from the largest software publisher in the world to run our US operation. That, and our clearly innovative dynamic documentation software had turned us into much more of a hot prospect.

Our current investors were keen that we find an additional investor to come in on round two at a higher share price than the original £1 per share. The weird arithmetic that applies in venture capital means that existing investors can mark up their original holding in a company if an independent third party is

willing to pay a higher price for the equivalent shares; the original book value of their shares can then be revalued to the new
price and they can then claim that they have achieved an
increase in the value of their portfolio, even though no real
money has yet been created.

We met with Syntech, a specialist IT venture capital
company run by Ken Barnes and David Thomson. Ken had
been a right-hand man to Kenneth Baker when he was UK
Minister for Information Technology, and used the network he
had gained there to effectively navigate the UK's technology
scene. His business partner, David Thomson, had a huge
amount of experience in developing technology business,
including having been appointed the first Operations Director
of the British Technology Group (BTG) with responsibility for
electronics and information technology projects, following
which he had been Chief Executive of Systems Programming
Ltd (SPL), one of the UK's largest software houses.

By an extraordinary coincidence, we discovered another
unexpected connection with David Thomson. As a boy, he had
been brought up in the very same pub next to Dalkeith Palace
that we'd all frequented for our boozy Friday lunchtimes, his
father being the publican there. Of course, this was many years
before we had become lunchtime regulars (and consumers of
their arcade games machine).

Syntech were very impressed with our business model and
keen to follow up. David Thomson led this process and we
finally agreed that they would invest at a price of £6 per share –
an impressive six times rise in the market valuation of the
company in only one year. The investors bought 52,551 new
CCPPOs at a price of £6 per share, raising £315,306 for the business. We converted our convertible shares, all 12,500 of them,
one-for-one for new ordinaries, and we created a new pot of
6,667 shares for Alan Boyd, in recognition of the value he had
'transferred' into the business. The result was that the investors

held 115,051 CCPPOs, or 67% of the company, and we retained 56,667 ordinaries, or 33% of the company.

We were now looking like a much more promising business than we had when we started, so we were able to take advantage of this by negotiating a performance 'ratchet', which had the effect that, if we were to deliver £500,000 profit by 1989/90 the equity structure would be changed, and we would own 54% of the equity. This was designed to give us an additional incentive to aggressively grow our business.

David Thomson agreed to join our board as a Non-Executive Director. His experience of growing previous UK technology businesses was very welcome.

We were off and running with our global plans – and OWL International Inc. was born in Bellevue, Washington.

It was the summer of 1985.

7

IT'S CALLED 'HYPERTEXT'

Alan Boyd had done some research and established that there already was a name for our technology – hypertext – and it had been first pioneered mainly by a phenomenal systems engineer called Doug Engelbart. The actual name, hypertext, came from a writer and visionary called Ted Nelson, based on ideas first described in an inspirational 1945 article by Professor Vannevar Bush of MIT.

Doug Engelbart had been inspired by an article by Bush, who had served as the US government's Chief Science Advisor during the Second World War. In the July 1945 issue of *The Atlantic* magazine, Bush speculated on the new technologies that would be developed in the post-war world, and he described a his concept for a machine he called the 'Memex'.

He wrote:

The human mind operates by association. With one item in its grasp, it snaps instantly to the next that is suggested by the association of thoughts, in accordance with some intricate web of trails carried by the cells of the brain. Whenever logical processes of thought are employed, there is an opportunity for a machine. Consider a future device for individual use which is a sort of mechanised private file and library. It needs a name, and, to coin one at random, 'memex' will do. A memex is a device in which an individual stores all his books, records, and communications, and which is mechanized so that it may be consulted with exceeding speed and flexibility. It is an enlarged intimate supplement to his memory.

He went on to describe how the user would operate his machine.

When the user is building a trail, he names it... before him are the two items to be joined, projected onto adjacent viewing positions... The user taps a single key, and the items are permanently joined... Thereafter, at any time, when one of these items is in view, the other can be instantly recalled merely by tapping a button.

A special button transfers him immediately to the first page of the index. Any given book of his library can thus be called up and consulted with far greater facility than if it were taken from a shelf. As he has several projection positions, he can leave one item in position while he calls up another. He can add marginal notes and comments... and it could even be arranged so that he can do this by a stylus scheme... just as though he had the physical page before him.

Of course, Bush's imaginary machine was just that – imaginary. He was writing at a time when electronic computing was in its infancy. A few primitive electronic calculation devices had been developed for wartime code-breaking, but the programmable computer was still a few years in the future.

Doug Engelbart was a young US Naval officer who read Bush's article in a Red Cross library in the Philippines while he was waiting to be returned to the USA after the defeat of Japan.

Bush's visionary machine inspired Engelbart's thinking after he returned to civilian life and eventually, in 1962, he wrote a technical paper (sending a copy to Vannevar Bush requesting his support) outlining how a computer could be used to implement some of Bush's ideas. He called the technique 'augmentation' as in 'augmenting human intellect' and he managed to win huge amounts of funding support to develop these ideas from the US government's Advanced Research Projects Agency (ARPA), the same agency that later funded the development of the ArpaNet, forerunner to the internet, and from NASA, the space agency.

Engelbart's NLS (oN Line System), developed by the Augmented Human Intellect Research Centre at the Stanford Research Institute (SRI), allowed users to create electronic interactive documents based on connected concepts, to create hierarchies of information and to collaborate with others on the joint development of documentation. This breakthrough work in personal computing was also responsible for the invention of many of the features we now recognise as standard in modern personal computer systems: notably text processing and electronic mail, multi-document screen displays and interactive control by the use of a pointing device. In a paper in 1963, Engelbart introduced, among other things, the device that later became known as the 'mouse'.

By 1968 Engelbart had built an effective demonstration system which utilised text and simple graphics driven by a keyboard and using his first ever computer mouse, which had been carved out of wood. Engelbart's mouse is now a featured exhibit in the Smithsonian Museum in Washington DC as a superb example of key breakthroughs in US technology.

At the Fall 1968 Joint Computer Conference[1] in December in San Francisco he demonstrated his oN Line System to an audience of computer engineers. In what has become known as 'The Mother of All Demos', he demonstrated a computer displaying an advanced graphics-based system in which linked information could be created and then triggered on the screen by pointing and clicking with his computer mouse. He moved from document to document with ease. In passing he also demonstrated electronic mail and teleconferencing features that enabled him to share the editing of documents with a colleague back in the SRI office in Palo Alto, around 30 miles away.

Engelbart's demonstration was based on very expensive computing power and high-bandwidth microwave links, and at that time could not be implemented in any way that was affordable for individuals, but it was undoubtedly a personal computer – a computer for personal use.

In the history of computer developments, it turned out, to a large extent, to be the forerunner for all today's personal computers such as the Apple Mac and Microsoft's Windows.

The other key individual in this story, Ted Nelson, was not an engineer but a visionary and futurologist who proposed his system, Xanadu, as the world's first 'hypertext' system, the name that he coined along with 'hypermedia':

> By 'hypertext' I mean non-sequential writing. Ordinary writing is sequential for two reasons. First, it grew out of speech . . . which (has) to be sequential, and second, because books are not convenient to read except in a sequence.
>
> But the structures of ideas are not sequential. They tie together every which way. And when we write we are always trying to tie things together in non-sequential ways.

Nelson's Xanadu was developed in conjunction with Andy van Dam of Brown University based in Rhode Island and was finally implemented on Sun workstations. It remained an fascinating research project but never emerged as a commercial product.

Nelson has always been somewhat critical of the World

Wide Web: while acknowledging its overwhelming success, he regarded it as too simplistic for the tasks it has been applied to. For example, Xanadu proposed a change management architecture which kept track of every version of a document and identified key factors such as copyright ownership.

Nelson was a much better proselytiser than engineer and he wrote a book, *Literary Machines*, which defined these concepts. He described his vision of a future where the individual could be driving along a highway and see a roadside building with a large, illuminated 'X' sign. This would be a Xanadu station, and you could stop there and pick up information, any information, for, in Ted Nelson's world, all the information in the world would be readily available at the click of a button at a Xanadu station.

Of course, that is a good description of the world we now live in today, except we don't need special buildings containing Xanadu stations, we just look up information on the smartphones and tablets that we carry with us.

Various other hypertext projects had been started around the USA, often inspired by Engelbart's innovations. Brown University in Rhode Island was the most advanced, but Carnegie Mellon and Xerox Parc were not far behind.

The March 1986 issue of *MacWorld* magazine contained a very comprehensive review on this subject. Jeffrey S Young, a founding editor of the magazine, wrote a well-researched feature called 'Hypermedia'. For the very first time in a popular publication, he told the whole hypertext story, from Vannevar Bush and Doug Engelbart to Ted Nelson, and he predicted that in a future Macintosh-like machine, people would routinely navigate documents and other media through a hypertext interface, pointing and clicking, to go from information to interlinked information.

He mentioned research activities at Brown, Stanford, MIT

and Carnegie Mellon, and in the labs at Apple, IBM, Xerox and AT&T. He reported that Norm Meyrowitz at Brown University had developed a prototype study aid called Intermedia for Shakespeare's *Romeo and Juliet* which linked text and commentary to video sections of the play. Young then speculated that although current Macintoshes might be too underpowered for such systems, future computers would undoubtedly have the ability to enable hypertext applications which could be used by a wide variety of users ranging from, he speculated, lawyers to creative artists.

What he didn't foresee was that the first version of our fully functional hypertext system – Guide – was to be launched for the Macintosh in only a few months' time, that August in fact, in an advertisement in his own magazine.

Other early developers in this field included Alan Kay, at Xerox PARC, who had speculated about a visionary device back in 1972, which he called a 'Dynabook'. It was to be a portable, tablet-like device, which he proposed could provide an excellent educational publishing device for children.

I remember seeing Alan Kay on the platform of a major US technology conference in the 1980s. He asked the audience, "How many of you have a personal computer?" and when all the hands went up – this being a technology conference – he said, "Great. Could you hold it up please", and of course nobody could comply. His point was that what we called a personal computer in those days was really an office computer and was located on your desk. It wasn't until sometime later that we had real personal computers in our bags or pockets.

Meanwhile, all these developments in interactive documentation had been largely unknown to Professor Peter Brown of the University of Kent at Canterbury on the other side of the Atlantic. Peter had, as I've described, independently created a system which had many of the characteristics of hypertext which, further developed by us to add complex layout display features and the key innovation of a hypertext link, went on to become the world's first commercially released hypertext system.

Our version of Guide for the Apple Mac, which we released in August 1986, had all the characteristics of a full-function hypertext system. It displayed documents made up of text displayed in multiple fonts with embedded images or graphics. Any piece of text and any area (or indeed sub-area) of a graphic could be turned into a hypertext button, and users would identify the buttons by the way that the computer pointer changed as they moved the mouse over the document. If the pointer turned into a 'crosshair' (a symbol that looked like a gunsight target) it meant that this was a stretch-text button with more document hidden underneath; if you clicked on a stretch-text button, the further information would be displayed and the cursor would turn into an open square which showed that if you clicked again at this point it could be 'folded' back under the button.

If the pointer turned into an asterisk cursor, it indicated a pop-up note or reference, and a right-arrow cursor indicated that this was a hypertext link and would take you to a different part of this document, or to another document entirely, which could be anywhere on your system, or indeed anywhere on your wider network.

As you changed the size and shape of individual windows on the screen the documents automatically changed shape to fit. There was no fixed page size so words and graphics automatically rewrapped to fill the window. As windows were resized to be smaller, images were intelligently scaled-down to a point, but not such that they became too small to be viewable. The user could quickly import documents and link them up to create a sophisticated hypertext collection of documents.

It was all there, and it worked like a dream on the early Apple Mac.

What we had developed was a completely novel way of publishing documents and interactive documents, on computer screens. And as we will see later, it made quite an impact.

———————————————————

1. Organised by the American Federation of Information Processing Societies (AFIPS).

8

SETTING UP IN SEATTLE

Once we had made the decision to hire Alan Boyd and open our own US office, the rest of 1985 and all of 1986 became a very busy time for the company. We were essentially forming the shape of the new OWL, our small business that would take on the world, starting with establishing our new sales and marketing function in the Seattle area.

Seattle is an attractive city in Washington State on the north-west corner of the United States. The Cascade Mountain range parallels the coast here and several of these mountains, such as Mount Si, Mount Rainier and Mount St Helens, are very large indeed. From some angles looking across the city from the north, Mount Rainier, although some 100 miles to the south, can still seem to loom large over the city.

The Seattle metropolitan area benefits not only by the views of these mountains but also by attractive bodies of water to the east and west. Inland of Seattle, Lake Washington separates the city from the eastside cities of Bellevue, Kirkland and Redmond, and offshore from Seattle the Olympic Peninsula traps a body of water named the Puget Sound which, although sea water, is much calmer than the open Pacific Ocean.

This whole western metropolitan area of Washington State has about the same population as Scotland, but even though it is geographically remote, tucked away at the top left-hand corner of the USA, its economy is a very dynamic one. As well as Boeing and Microsoft, over the years Starbucks, Costco and Amazon have all built impressive global businesses after being first established there.

We decided to set up OWL International Inc. in the eastside city of Bellevue. Our first presence was a serviced office in the downtown Plaza Centre at 10900 8th Street NE which Alan Boyd told me was the same building in which Bill Gates and Paul Allen had started Microsoft ten years or so before. Would that be a good omen, I wondered? We had a single office space but we could make use of the meeting rooms and the office copier, and our telephone would be answered as if it were our own office.

Alan took over all of our US dealings concerning live projects such as PadLock (our latest name for our copy protection system), InPrint (document production) and Logian (expert systems) but he was really getting his teeth into Guide. Our objective was still to have Guide published by a third-party software publishing company, so he was contacting various candidates and demonstrating the product.

While we were negotiating for Alan to join us, we had had various meetings with the Scottish Development Agency and during one of these meetings we came up with the idea of running a one-day conference for the Scottish software industry, bringing them a range of topical information and intelligence from the US West Coast software publishing scene. Alan would use his extensive contacts to identify them and persuade them to come over, attracting them with a free trip to Edinburgh.

We assembled a stellar programme, including Nigel Smith of GSS to speak about OEM marketing (an OEM, or original equipment manufacturer, is a company that obtains and resells components acquired from third-party developers), Chris Morgan of Lotus to talk on market communication, Vijay Vashee, responsible for the key project planning product at Microsoft, to talk about product marketing and retail distribution, and Maggie Cannon, the editor of the leading industry trade weekly *InfoWorld*, to talk about press and media relations.

We held this conference at the Edinburgh Sheraton and it was very successful. For most of the audience much of the content was more aspirational than practical, but it turned out to be extremely valuable to us as we contemplated the transition of our small Edinburgh-based technology business into a player on the global software scene.

Alan and I decided to attend the Comdex '85 conference in late November to make contacts and take the pulse of the state of the industry. Unlike back in 1983, when I spent the time wandering among the various exhibition stands, this time I was accompanied by Alan who, as an experienced professional, introduced me to the way in which Comdex really works – it is not pounding the floor at the exhibition halls during the day that counts, but rather attending the right parties in the evenings. If you get an invite to the key receptions (or indeed gate-crash them, which isn't difficult as most of them don't have security and are held in accessible huge banqueting halls) you get to chat to industry executives in a more informal setting, and this is where the real business is done.

One of the more exclusive parties that you did need to have a ticket to get into was thrown by Apple Computer in a Las Vegas nightclub, where we were entertained by the Commodores, one of the top bands of the day. This was, of course, a deliberately ironic choice as Commodore was at the time a brand of early personal computer in competition with Apple.

Finally, in the late evening, we rocked up to a penthouse suite that Alan knew about, to join the real senior movers and shakers of the industry. Despite the reputation of Las Vegas as a party city these were pretty tame events, but the bath was filled to the brim with ice and beer bottles and the attendees talked endlessly about computer developments.

It wasn't very 'Rock and Roll'; Comdex had a fairly poor reputation amongst the Las Vegas casino owners. Most of the computer geeks didn't gamble, feeling, like me, that just trying to make a living in high tech was gambling enough.

Following Comdex, we finally concluded that we should publish the software ourselves, under our own brand name. Alan had persuaded us that with his network of contacts in the industry, distributors and press, he could successfully launch our product and make a significant impact. It seemed a bit crazy to me as I couldn't believe it could be that easy, but he was very confident that we could pull it off and we decided to go ahead.

We also moved to our own first 'proper' office with our own front door. It was a mile or so away from the central Bellevue business district at 14218 NE 21st Street. The space was in a line of small single-storey offices behind a low-rise strip of retail businesses, and Alan had hired a technology support guy, Dave Coffman, and an administration assistant.

Meanwhile, having made the decision to publish Guide ourselves, we set about turning it into a software package for release on the Apple Macintosh. We hired Bill Hill, then a journalist on *The Scotsman* and a hobbyist tech enthusiast, to write our user manual. We didn't realise then that we had spotted a future star; in later years, Bill left journalism to work as a manager for Adobe in Edinburgh and eventually was hired by

Microsoft in Redmond to manage all their typefaces and font management businesses.

The manual Bill wrote was pretty good, but to make sure it was the right international standard we also got it sub-edited by an experienced American documentation specialist, Steve Lambert, who had been responsible for several user manuals at Microsoft as well as editing books at Microsoft Press.

Our software packaging was to give no indication of its Scottish origin. Alan believed that our manuals should be printed on US-sized paper and use American English, and the registration card was to be posted back to our Bellevue office. To our customers, we were to look in all respects like any other West Coast American software company.

The Guide package

When it came to determining the terms and conditions for our software package Alan joked that we should adopt what he called the 'Kodak guarantee' in our software package. When I looked puzzled, he explained that it meant: 'If this film kills you, we'll replace the cost of the film.'

We hired John Jerome, who with his business partner, Jim Kirby, ran a design business called Parallel Communications in nearby Kirkland to design our logo, packaging and advertisements. Our new logo showed an image of an owl in profile as if swooping down on its prey, its wings splattered with colour and the name OWL below, the 'W' taking the form of a hand-drawn crayon swoop.

The logo was attractive, original and had an effective contemporary look, and we adopted it for all our stationery, business cards and packaging.

In March 1986, Microsoft decided to hold a key three-day conference at the Seattle Sheraton focussed on the technology of CD-ROMs, the new format of digital disks that was beginning to be built into computers. Low-cost CD-ROMs could store around 650 megabytes of data, substantially more than other technology at the time, and Microsoft wanted to ensure that CD-ROMs became a standard feature of future PCs. This conference was intended by Microsoft to kick-start the industry in building products and applications to exploit this new format.

The conference opened with veteran educator Gabriel Ofiesh giving a presentation entitled 'The Seamless Carpet of Knowledge and Learning' in which he made extensive reference to Vannevar Bush's 1945 article, 'As We May Think', in *The Atlantic*, the very article which had so influenced Doug Engelbart; this article was also reprinted in full at the front of the conference's accompanying book.

Alan's contacts within Microsoft ensured that we were able to have Peter Brown included on the programme as a speaker. His presentation was called 'Viewing Documents on a Screen'. He demonstrated a version of our hypertext system, which we had redubbed 'CD Guide' to fit with the theme of the conference, our system being, we claimed, ideal for developing large, complex hypertext publications which could then be published on CD-ROMs. This presentation was the first time we had publicly talked about Guide, and we attracted a lot of attention from various attendees, winning us quite a few leads, including from Boeing and Schlumberger.

One promising lead, it turned out, was from Hewlett-Packard (HP), who were investigating how they were going to build a project for the Ford Motor Company in Dearborn, Michigan, to develop a system designed to deliver online electronic service manuals in a project called Service Bay Diagnostic System (SBDS). HP were interested in investigating whether we could provide the online documentation technology, and they in turn would build the ruggedised computers built into a sturdy industrial trolley that could be moved around an automobile service bay and plugged into individual cars to obtain diagnostic information and display detailed technical maintenance manuals.

The system they envisaged was a pretty sophisticated use of hypertext technology. The technical manuals were to be distributed on CD-ROMs but users were also going to get regular updates by floppy disk or by connection to a server via a built-in modem, and the user was to experience a seamless experience without being aware of whether the section of the manual was coming from the CD-ROM or from a subsequent update.

We had already started working on an implementation of

Guide for early development versions of Microsoft Windows and we reckoned that we were the only company in the world that could do all of what Ford and HP needed in a cost-effective way.

This looked reasonably promising. We still hadn't released our first product and we were already talking with two of the world's biggest corporations, Ford Motor Company and Hewlett-Packard, about a bespoke system to meet their needs.

IT WAS around this time that we came to the conclusion that our involvement with the Alvey Programme, the consortium working on new publishing technology that we had signed up to back when we were first setting up, was turning out to be far too unimaginative and frustrating – an unnecessary diversion from our growing commercial activities. It had become clear that GEC, the consortium leaders, were only interested in getting one of their pedestrian existing projects funded and weren't remotely interested in recognising any innovation in the publishing technologies that we were proposing to bring to the programme.

Attending all the project meetings was a tedious waste of time so I decided to meet with Brian Oakley, the senior civil servant who oversaw the programme, and told him of our intention to withdraw from the consortium. He wasn't happy.

We had hired a part-time PR consultant, Emrys Inker, to manage our press relations with the UK media. Emrys's day job was running the PR department at the Scottish Development Agency, so he was very well placed to know about, and to place us in front of, any technology journalist who came to Scotland or showed interest in the Scottish scene. We paid him a small retainer and he crafted our various press releases and advised on how to get the best coverage.

In most cases we learned that the best way to get good coverage was to persuade one individual newspaper or magazine to do a substantial feature on an exclusive basis. The *Financial Times* and *The Sunday Times* were always our favourite target but sometimes we would also deal with the UK trade press, which were then *Computing* and *Computer Weekly*.

So, when we decided to pull out of the Alvey Programme we put out a press release. It got quite extensive coverage in the trade press. It didn't endear us to the UK technology establishment, and certainly not to the Alvey directorate, but in the longer term I believe that that we gained some respect. Most people know what a waste of time many publicly funded consortiums are, and we were seen to be making a sensible decision in the circumstances.

Ironically, when we won the BCS Award for Innovation a few years later, in 1988, it was Brian Oakley, the then President of the BCS, who introduced us at the ceremony at the Royal Society. That seemed proof enough that we had been very innovative after all.

BACK IN THOSE DAYS, communication between Edinburgh and Bellevue was quite primitive. We bought two fax machines, one for each office, but most of the communication was by phone between 4pm and 6pm (when it was 8am to 10am in Bellevue); there were typically several calls underway between our offices.

Brian Newton, one of the talented software engineers we had hired from ICL, set about building an office email system from public domain software. He established an email service for each of our offices and built an automatic 'bot' that used the commercial service CompuServe to link the two. It automatically accessed CompuServe every hour through the day, but in addition between 4pm and 8pm UK time it did it every 10 minutes, to clear the emails posted by OWL staff in both offices. This was a huge improvement – we could now conduct an effective email conversation between our premises.

Our friend Derek Gray called by to introduce us to an opportunity at Apple Computer. He was doing a lot of work with them in promoting Aldus PageMaker and had built up a close relationship. Indeed, his work in developing desktop publishing with Apple in the UK was later adopted as a global marketing push across the whole corporation.

Apple Computer's operations across Europe consisted of sales offices with very few technical staff and they were looking to appoint an organisation who could provide frontline technical support to the various software developers scattered across Europe, to distribute development kits issued by Apple's HQ in Cupertino, and to provide first-level support to European companies developing Macintosh software.

We were clearly a leading developer of software for the Apple Macintosh and so we bid for, and then won, the contract. We set up a small administrative team in our Edinburgh office which would regularly receive development disks and documentation arriving from Cupertino; we would duplicate them locally and send on these development packs to the various companies which had signed up for Apple support across Europe. Although this could be seen as a diversion from our main activities, we decided that it would enable us to build a stronger relationship with Apple Computer.

We were not to know what would happen later.

WE WERE CLOSING in on early September, the release date for our Guide product for the Apple Mac. The main product, Guide, allowed the author full control over the editing process required to create sophisticated hypertext documents.

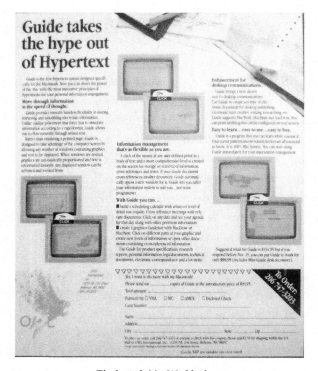

The launch MacWorld advert

In order to enable Guide to be used effectively as a publishing system, we included in the package a complementary product called Guide Envelope, which could be used to make a standalone hypertext document which bundled together both the document and the technology to read it in one stand-alone mini-application. Once you had created a hypertext document with Guide, you could then use Envelope to distribute it to anybody without restriction, and they could read, but not change, the document.

Guide was finally launched in an advertisement in the September 1986 edition of *Macworld* magazine (which came out in August).

The advert was headed 'Guide takes the hype out of Hypertext'.

Of course, our intention was the exact opposite – we wanted to create as much hype as possible around our product.

The original product for the Macintosh was advertised at $134.95 with a launch promotional price of $99.95 valid until November 15th. It would work on a Macintosh 512K, and we strongly recommended a second disk drive, otherwise there would be a great deal of mounting and unmouting the disks in and out of the single built-in disk drive.

The product was released. We were off and running.

Actually, for what it was worth, we were now the leading – indeed, the only – commercial hypertext company in the world.

Of course, at that time, hypertext was still what is known in the tech industry as a 'zero million dollar' market.

9

BUILDING A HYPERTEXT FUTURE

Over the next few months we picked up a number of small pilot contracts from the likes of Schlumberger, Gestetner and Letraset. We created a hypertext online manual to be shipped with Aldus PageMaker 2.0 and we created some PostScript 'type effects' products for Derek Gray at McQueens which allowed users to create various artistic renderings of standard PostScript fonts to be inserted into documents.

On 7 October 1986 the senior management team of OWL decamped to Pitlochry Hydro for an off-site strategy session. Scottish hydros are grand old sandstone-built resorts erected in Victorian times; the name 'hydro' referring to the fact that the water in the surrounding area was thought to be rich in hydrogen and beneficial to health.

But we chose it because, in October, it was really cheap.

Many of these Scottish hydros have excellent sport and fitness facilities, but the only thing we could find for physical activity in the Pitlochry Hydro was a lonely table tennis table. They didn't even have a swimming pool. Still, it meant our discussions were not distracted.

The main decision agreed at this strategy session was that we should focus on being 'the hypertext company', dropping distracting activities such as our copy protection technology, and that we should primarily use our packaged product, Guide, as a shop window to demonstrate our hypertext skills. We hoped this would lead to us being commissioned to build customised solutions for the OEM market. An OEM company – such as Dell or Hewlett-Packard – doesn't develop much of the software that they ship with their computers; they acquire it from independent suppliers.

This turned out to be a wise strategic decision and it went on to drive our business over the coming years.

Our first OEM project, which was with Hewlett-Packard for Ford, was developing very nicely. We were well advanced in creating a version of Guide for Microsoft Windows, which HP would use as the basis for the SBDS system. The demands of the Ford system allowed us to build some great features into Guide, funded by their project.

As an example of this, the basic sets of manuals were to be delivered on CD-ROMs, but regular updates were to be transmitted over modems and our system was to seamlessly update the manuals, so the end user wasn't aware whether the technical information being displayed was from the CD-ROM or from a downloaded update. The version viewed by the user was always up to date.

In the same year, 1987, we developed a major hypertext project for the British Library in conjunction with a major exhibition they were holding, and in the May, we launched our first version of Guide on Microsoft Windows (1.04 version), a buggy operating system which was barely functional. Following our experience with Aldus we also released a variant of Guide for the creation of online 'help' systems for other companies to include with their software releases, which we called Guidance. The first foreign-language variant, a French version of Guide, came out that year too. We had also picked up a contract from Advanced Memory Systems to develop a desktop publishing system for them.

Lynda Hardman, the Development Manager for Guide products, asked to see me and informed me that what she really wanted to do was new computing research and I explained that, at that time, we could not afford a research function and had to concentrate on commercialising, as best we could, the existing research of Peter Brown's work at the University of Kent.

So she went off for a while to become an academic researcher at Heriot-Watt and Edinburgh universities in the Artificial Intelligence and Scottish Human-Computer Interface (HCI) Centre. A couple of years later she returned to OWL, by which time we were larger and had developed a need to contribute to research activities. By then it had become important for us to be involved in standards development, and Lynda played a key role in contributing to the Dexter Hypertext Reference Model as part of a National Institute of Standards and Technology (NIST) standards workshop, and the European Hyperate project. (After OWL was sold, Lynda went on to build a substantial academic research career with CWI in Amsterdam; she was appointed an ACM (Association for Computing Machinery) Distinguished Scientist in 2014 and became the President of Informatics Europe in 2016.)

WE HIRED Alister Gibson to take a business development role. He was a young Scot who had completed an MBA at the University of Sheffield and had become a business support officer at the SDA, where he had been assigned to be our liaison officer. We had become sufficiently impressed with each other that he agreed to leave the SDA and join us at OWL.

Shortly after Alister arrived in January 1987, we shipped him and Robbie McLaren off to 'work the booth' at the MacWorld trade show in San Francisco.

They flew into Seattle and the next morning Alan Boyd, John Nelson, Robbie and Alister loaded up a truck with our trade show booth and headed off on the drive south down I-5 for the 18-hour journey to the Moscone Center in downtown San Francisco.

The keynote at this show was delivered by Apple's CEO John Sculley on the subject of 'intelligent documents', where he speculated on the emergence of computer-delivered documents that could carry more information than could just be shown on a page. He didn't mention us, but it seemed he was talking about our kind of technology.

The MacWorld show at that time was a cross between Hollywood and an Apple cult-like experience. Excitable Apple fans rubbed shoulders with stars of California's music and movie communities. Some of the better-known celebrities garnered huge crowds of fans as they made their way around the show floor.

On the first day, Herbie Hancock and his entourage paid a visit to our booth, but the real highlight came on the second day. The A-list actor and comedian Robin Williams stopped by and saw Robbie demo a Guide version of a Robert Burns poem, where we had employed hypertext links to show pop-up translations of the Scots words. After a quick run-though, Robin Williams took control of the mouse and proceeded to read Burns in a Scottish accent, followed by Burns in the kind of tinny electronic voice a computer might use and finally he combined the two and gave a fabulous performance of the poem as if delivered by a Scottish computer.

That kind of endorsement you just can't buy. By the end of the first day, Guide was in the top 10 bestselling Mac software packages.

Alan still had good connections in the music industry from his days as a roadie for the likes of Janis Joplin, and one night after the MacWorld show they all went to a party at musician Todd Rundgren's house in downtown San Francisco. Todd at that time was in a relationship with Babe Buell, a former Playboy playmate of the month, and many of the party attendees were either long-haired rocker types or statuesque, scantily clad models.

Alister recalls standing in the kitchen, surrounded by $1,000-worth of sushi and a dozen or so models. This was his first trip to the USA and was an experience he was never going to forget.

Also, that January, we got tipped off that the *New York Times* was to print an article on hypertext, inspired by the journalist's experience of Guide. Back in 1987 the *New York Times* covered personal computer topics only once each week in a column published in their Tuesday 'Science Times' section. The time difference between Seattle and New York is three hours, and the national edition of the *Times*, which is printed overnight in New York, is printed on the West Coast mid-evening and distributed that night.

And so, late in the evening of Monday, 12th January 1987, I was lurking near a *New York Times* vending box waiting for the next morning's edition of the paper to be delivered. When I got my copy, I turned to that week's 'Personal Computing' column written by Erik Sandberg-Diment. He wrote about the concept of hypertext, referring to Vannevar Bush, Ted Nelson, Doug Engelbart... and Peter Brown. At the end of this article, he moved on to introduce Guide, which he said, 'suggests some truly intriguing possibilities'. He concluded by saying he would

> *continue this discussion next week, if I can locate the various weighty cogent thoughts I filed away deep down among the many layers of Guide.*

This was much better than we could have dreamed of. Not only did he write about Guide in this column, but he was also going to write about it again in next week's column; we had two weeks in a row devoted to us in the only weekly column about personal computing in the *New York Times* – how cool was that.

The next Tuesday, 20th January, in an article headed 'Hazy Maze of Buttons', Sandberg-Diment wrote extensively about his experience in using Guide. He acknowledged that the system was very powerful and ideal for building technical manuals or help systems, but he seemed to have got lost in the flexible nature of his particular hypertext documents, creating too complex a document and, to some extent, getting 'lost in hyperspace'. In fairness, this was a real issue – mostly solved by making the effort to build in good navigation techniques.

Over the next few months, we received more great coverage in the trade and technical press. The April 1987 issue of *Byte* magazine carried not one but two short reviews in the columns by Bruce Webster and Ezra Shapiro. Shapiro wrote 'on the whole, I am enthusiastic about Guide' and went on to speculate that it would be ideal for managing huge volumes of documentation on CD-ROMs. His slight reticence was probably because this was novel software and it took some people time to get used to how powerful it was, and how to use it well.

Bruce Webster chose it as his 'Product of the Month'. Webster clearly spent more time working with the product and identified several features which assisted navigation and mitigated the 'lost in hyperspace' problem. These included a back-track icon; a 'top level' feature which returned the document to its original state, and a 'show symbols' command which bracketed each button so they could be quickly identified. He concluded:

> *Guide easily earns its award as product of the month on three different counts: innovative application, excellent software (I have*

yet to run across a single bug), and high-quality documentation. It is proof... that the best, most innovative software being developed today is being done on the Macintosh.

In later columns, star contributor Jerry Pournelle wrote about Guide in his June 1987 'Chaos Manor' *Byte* column:

The program works smoothly, it's easy to use, and unique as far as I know. If you do presentations, or you're just interested in organising information, you'll want to look at Guide. Highly recommended.

In passing, Pournelle also made reference in his article to visiting our suite at a CD-ROM conference and being delighted to find it was stocked with several single-malt Scotch whiskies. Pournelle wrote in his column,

When I asked about the notorious Scottish weather, Robbie McLaren, product manager, said 'Och, it keeps the programmers inside and working. Now if we could only keep them away from the whisky'. Having been to Edinburgh, I quite understand.

For some time, I had implemented a company policy whereby every time any employee travelled from Edinburgh to our Seattle office, they were instructed to buy a bottle of good-quality single malt whisky at the duty-free section of the airport – reimbursable on their expense claim – and to put the bottle into a cupboard at the Bellevue office. Whenever we attended a technical conference, we would rent a suite somewhere in the hotel and became notorious, certainly among the journalists, for our informal whisky-tasting sessions.

I recall at a later conference waiting for an elevator. When the door opened Jerry Pournelle was standing there, and he was quick off the mark: "Oh wow, I didn't realise you guys were here – what's your suite number?"

Alan had hired a small, grey, balding, somewhat dishevelled older guy called Wes Thomas to handle our press coverage and enable our interactions at trade shows. He had a very impressive 'black book' of connections and somehow or other, he knew his way to all the right senior contacts, both in the industry and within the press. He operated in tandem with his daughter Karen, a somewhat aloof five-foot curvy platinum blonde in vertiginous heels, who would cooly and efficiently handle all the detailed arrangements for each meeting.

As well as the coverage in the more informal multi-topic *Byte* columns by Shapiro, Webster and Pournelle, we also got a full formal product review in the October 1987 edition of *Byte* by William Hersey. He concluded:

> *The product points the way to future 'hypermedia' systems that will link animated video and sound with massive text and graphics files. For now, Guide is an affordable, highly functional program that will let you dabble in hypertext – and maybe get your points across more effectively.*

We also got a full product review by Michael Antebi in the 22nd June edition of *InfoWorld* magazine, the leading US trade weekly for the personal computing industry. He praised the program, the documentation, the lack of bugs and the technical support, but said, justifiably, that to create large hypertext publications required a level of planning in advance. He concluded:

> *Guide is unique in the world of personal computers and, as such, is an invaluable program. We think Guide's application goes well beyond the obvious.*

After all these reactions from the trade and general press, we had definitely arrived. Our product had made quite an impact.

10

A BUMP IN THE ROAD

I n March 1987 I began to get hints from people I knew at Apple Computer that an issue was developing. We were told off-the-record to watch out for an application that was scheduled to be published by Apple at some time that autumn.

Bill Atkinson, a key software architect at Apple who was responsible for the development of the core graphics architecture of the Macintosh, along with its revolutionary MacPaint program, had been busy developing an easy-to-use application development package which he had called WildCard.

Steve Jobs had suddenly left Apple in 1985 after losing the support of its Board of Directors, and John Sculley, a marketing man who had made his name building the Pepsi soft drinks business, had taken over as CEO. Sculley was a salesman who was famously non-technical, so Atkinson's status in the company was high. In the absence of the founders, Jobs and Wozniac, he was regarded as one of the top technical gurus in the company.

As a condition of Apple publishing WildCard, Atkinson insisted that his program become ubiquitous by being effectively given away unrestricted. He wanted to ensure that there was no barrier to the use of his tool and any applications developed on it and he reasoned that WildCard could also boost demand for Apple Macintoshes by allowing users to quickly create simple new applications.

Somebody at Apple slipped us an unofficial pre-release copy of WildCard in early June 1987. We examined it carefully, Robbie McLaren in particular went through its features very thoroughly, and we came to the conclusion that it really wasn't a competitor to Guide. It seemed to us that WildCard was clearly an application development tool; indeed, Bill Atkinson himself had described it as a "software erector set".

It enabled authors to create sets of fixed format cards (sized to fit the Macintosh's then 9-inch black and white screen) made up of text and graphics with an easy-to-use scripting language which could be triggered by clicking on hotspots in the cards. It would enable people without programming skills to quickly create simple applications.

We were reassured that this really didn't look like much of a threat.

What we didn't know then was the market positioning that would be chosen by Apple for this program, and the fact that it would be given away effectively for free.

It transpired that for copyright reasons the name 'Wild-Card' could not be used, and a new name was chosen. They decided to call it Hypercard, since among its features it implemented a form of hypertext link to connect sets of cards.

Three companies, Authorware, Course Builder and ourselves, were invited down to a meeting at Apple's headquarters at Cupertino in July 1987. We three had been selected because Apple executives thought that Hypercard might have most impact on sales of our products.

Apple executive Bud Colligan gave us an introduction to Hypercard – he didn't know that we had already had an informal pre-release version which we had carefully studied. He offered to help us in re-targeting our market positioning to mitigate any damage that Hypercard would do to us.

Apple had worked hard to encourage innovative third-party developers to create breakthrough software for the Macintosh and a few of the managers in their evangelist function were clearly embarrassed by this development of a package that potentially competed with existing third-party products.

Hypercard was finally released in August 1987 and Apple spent a reported $12 million on its launch, including taking out a 12-page supplement in the *Wall Street Journal* on the day it was released, and we were shocked when we read how this new product was identified. Their positioning was identical to ours, almost a word-for-word copy of our marketing materials. It told the story of Vannevar Bush, Ted Nelson and Doug Engelbart and pitched the product as a hypertext development tool. We were sure that this had never been the intention of Atkinson, but the Apple marketing people had taken over and they had clearly decided that the hypertext positioning was one that they could aggressively push.

Then we discovered to our horror the other key piece of information. Although it was notionally priced at $49, Apple were going to bundle Hypercard with all new Macintoshes and users would be free to pass it on to their friends. Not only that, if you went to an Apple store with a blank disk, they would copy Hypercard onto it for free.

This seemed to be a major disaster for us. Apple were positioning Hypercard as a hypertext system and were giving it away to anybody who wanted it. Not surprisingly, sales of Guide for the Macintosh dried up immediately and over the coming weeks retailers and distributors were returning unsold copies of the program to us.

We might have been able to somehow compete against a

paid-for product, but we really couldn't be expected to compete with free.

Suddenly, because of Apple's vast marketing power, we were no longer 'the hypertext company'. Overnight, Apple had stolen this position.

Our Sales Manager in Bellevue, Barb Landis, told *Computer-World* magazine that OWL was planning a conversion program, codenamed 'William Tell', to take Hypercard files from Macintoshes and convert them to Guide documents for Macs or PCs. This story had been cooked up between her and Alan Boyd without reference to anybody in Edinburgh.

In fact, we had no intention of doing anything of the kind.

Hypercard really wasn't a hypertext system. Indeed, its modern equivalent, a system-independent development environment called LiveCode, is based closely on Hypercard and is used widely in education to give young people a first experience in coding applications.

Fortunately, we had already launched a version of Guide to run on an early release of Microsoft Windows, which had turned out to be an extremely challenging task because the underlying MS Windows system at that time was extremely fragile. The struggle to get a first working version of Guide on the embryonic Windows 1.0 platform had Brian Newton banging his head against a wall for the best part of six months. He particularly struggled with the Windows font management system and blew up at one point with a tantrum because he just couldn't do it. It wasn't his fault, and all the faulty interfaces were reported to Microsoft.

Brian was an interesting character. He was a superb software engineer and in his aging Saab car he had all the seats removed except for the driver's – he enjoyed his own company and really didn't want to be asked to give lifts to others.

When it emerged that Microsoft had made such a shambles of the font management in Windows 1.0, Robbie McLaren, the

Product Marketing Manager for the release, decreed that in the first release of Guide for Windows, you could have any font you liked – so long as it was Arial.

Taking the choice out was the masterstroke that saved the day and saved that product release.

That and subsequent development work by John Briggs and Duncan Muirhead, two skilled developers who had joined us from ICL Dalkeith, laid the Windows software foundations that pretty much all our subsequent software sales were built on. The work of our development team to create that first well-engineered Windows product was key to the company's ongoing success.

We launched our version of Guide for Microsoft Windows v1.4 in May 1987. Compared to the Macintosh, where the graphics performance had been built into the fundamental design of the computer, Microsoft Windows ran on top of PCs which had never really been designed to handle powerful, sophisticated graphics. It is fair to say that Guide on Windows was pretty clunky compared to the Macintosh version, however the program itself worked well enough to be used to build and deliver hypertext documents.

At that time, 95% of the personal computers sold in the world for business use were PCs and only about 5% of the market were Macintoshes. Apple were throwing lots of money at promoting the Apple Macintosh and their Hypercard software, but for any PC user who wanted to try out such techniques we were the only people they could turn to.

The whole episode was a very disruptive experience. Our Macintosh market had disappeared overnight, but in the longer term our market on Microsoft Windows had received a superb boost from the huge amount of money being spent by Apple to educate the market about the benefits of hypertext.

AS WE RAN Apple's European developer's support under contract from Apple Inc., we regularly received master copies of manuals and software kits from Cupertino which we would arrange to have locally reprinted for distribution to developers across Europe.

One day in late 1987, after the Hypercard launch, Gordon Simpson, who ran this unit within OWL, came to me with a page from an Apple developer's manual that had just arrived from California. This page showed a developer's screenshot from an Apple Mac which showed several programs on its desktop. One of these programs was an early pre-release version of WildCard (later released as Hypercard) but alongside this on the same desktop was a copy of a pre-release version of Guide 2.0 which hadn't yet, at that time, been published.

Whenever we issued pre-release versions of our programs to potential partners, we always labelled them with a unique identification code, and obtained a non-disclosure agreement (NDA) signed by the recipient. This copy of Guide 2.0 had such an identification code on it, but it was not one that had been licensed to Apple, indeed we had never supplied a pre-release copy of Guide 2.0 to Apple.

This copy of our software had obviously been obtained unofficially and technically Apple had no right to own or use it. One of the new features of Guide 2.0 was a new, simple, embedded coding language in which a user could write extra functions which then could be triggered by pressing a newly developed 'command' button, and as WildCard had a similar function, we had to assume that the WildCard developers might have been examining our feature as an example of such a mechanism as they developed their product.

I contacted Apple to bring this to their attention and ask for an explanation of where they had got this program. From that moment on all meetings with Apple were accompanied by lawyers – lots of lawyers.

Eventually, on 28th January 1988, we were called back down to Cupertino to try and resolve the issue. I was accompanied by Bill Nisen, who was helping us in Bellevue and was very experienced in software publishing (he had even written a book about it). There were five Apple executives ranged against us, including a couple of their internal lawyers.

"How much damage has Apple releasing Hypercard inflicted on your business?" we were asked. Our previous year's published accounts, which we could be sure Apple would have seen, had shown our revenue that year as £564,477, but a huge chunk of that was contract business based on our Microsoft Windows technology. In truth, our sales of the Guide product on the Apple Mac had been modest, not least because sales of the Mac at that stage had also been modest.

We did some calculations, added in consequential damage, added loss of future earnings and doubled the resulting figure, "About $200,000", we declared.

We were asked to leave the room briefly, but within a few minutes we were called back. "OK. We'll pay you $200,000."

Rats!

That was far too easy. Clearly, we should have asked for much more.

Of course, throughout all this time that we were complaining that it was absolutely appalling that Apple had obtained an unauthorised pre-release copy of our program we never ever admitted to them that we had in fact similarly acquired an unauthorised pre-release copy of their program.

We took their money.

11

ATTRACTING ATTENTION

During 1987, we were attracting the attention of others. Steve Jobs, after being ejected from Apple, had started a new company called NeXT, in which he proposed a powerful workstation-like computer system that would run the latest version of Unix. As Apple had launched the Macintosh with a team of 'evangelists' dedicated to encouraging attractive applications to be developed and published for their platform, we'd been told that NeXT was doing something similar.

Alan Boyd and I had been invited to visit NeXT and get a briefing on their new machine. Just as when Alan had shown me the pre-released Macintosh in a locked room at Microsoft, NeXT was infected by Jobs's paranoid position about the secrecy of his products prior to release, so we were shown some boxes covered by an all-enveloping cloth, which they claimed was their breakthrough system. As we didn't get to see anything of their proposed system this meeting turned out to be pointless. We left perplexed.

Our project with HP and Ford on their Service Bay Diagnostic System was attracting attention from other automotive manufacturers. In April 1987 I was contacted by Bernard Pergamin, an executive at Renault in Paris. He had been experimenting with Guide and thought it had potential for delivering his online documentation needs.

I flew to Paris to meet with Pergamin and discuss his project. Renault was at the time an IBM customer and so it wasn't long before this project attracted the attention of IBM, whose European headquarters were also in Paris. I was invited back to meet up with them.

My meeting was at the IBM Europe headquarters in the La Défense area of Paris. After security entry checks (which was relatively unusual in those days) I was ushered into a large room where about 20 executives gathered for my demonstration of Guide on Windows. They seemed impressed with what they saw, and I found myself quickly attached to two key IBM individuals: Charles de Testa, a French software engineer who spoke excellent English, and Tom Pate, an American who was the IBM sales lead for the automotive sector in Europe.

I had always been worried about the lack of traditional sales skills in our company and I had hired Ken Naismith as our Sales Manager. Ken was a rather different animal to the rest of our technology-trained employees. He didn't have a university degree, but he had, to me, something much more valuable, having been trained as a salesman while working at Xerox, one of the most successful sales-oriented companies around.

The week that Ken arrived, he and I set off for Paris to meet with Pergamin, IBM Europe, and IBM France. It was also an opportunity for me to get to know him better. As well as the business meetings, we talked at length over dinner and even managed to take in a show at the Moulin Rouge, although we surmised that the performance was perhaps performed by the 'B' team as the dancers tended to bump into each other while performing their dance routines.

Ken quickly became very effective in the company. We still

followed our policy that, if possible, any significant customer visit should be manned by two of us. Ken was frequently paired up with software engineers who could manage the technology but were too mild-mannered to ask for the business.

Ken did that bit – closing the deals.

The work with HP's Service Bay Diagnostic System for Ford in Detroit led to a project with Ford of Europe's Advanced Business Organisation in Cologne. In one meeting, Ken was discussing money, as usual, at one end of the table with Ford's Dietmar Olefs, and Phil Cooke was down the other end next to Gert Schwartz, who was a systems expert seconded to Ford from a dealership and a very practical man, who could 'see through a brick wall, given time', as they say.

He leaned towards Phil and said in a low voice: "Phil, I wish I had your job; you're just making this up as you go along, aren't you?"

Of course, he was right. No one had built this kind of technology before, but we were pretty confident that we could invent the future of online engineering publishing, and indeed we did.

If we had only known how little we knew, we would probably not have achieved half as much as we did. The partnership between Ken, our salesman, and whichever engineer happened to be accompanying him began to really work well.

Ken told me that a "not insignificant piece of work" remark from an engineer like Gordon Dougan was an indication that he could demand £30,000 or so of business. He quickly got the hang of packaging up our opportunities into proposed development proposals and then closing the sale.

The solutions engineers learned to arrange overseas trips without getting Ken's lack of administration skills involved, but on one occasion Ken booked a visit to a prospect in Germany, in a little place called Neubeckum. Ken and Phil flew into

Dusseldorf with 'plenty of time' – according to Ken – to make the appointment.

However, when they checked the map in the hire car at the start of our journey, Neubeckum turned out to be 80 miles away. Ken was infamous for his speed on the M8 between Glasgow and Edinburgh, but it was as nothing to what he managed on the autobahn with no speed limits to constrain him even vaguely. Even at speeds of well over 100mph, they failed spectacularly to make the meeting on time.

They arrived eventually at a cement works. The prospective customer turned out to have no significant development budget, and nothing more was said about, or heard from, them ever again. That was the one that got away.

Our relationship with IBM was developing strongly. I was twice invited down to visit IBM Research Labs at Hursley, near Winchester, to meet with their teams developing their advanced displays and their OS/2 operating system.

I also followed up an invitation to meet with Wendy Hall, a lecturer at the nearby University of Southampton who at that time was leading a research programme into new electronic publishing techniques.

(Wendy later became a very influential person in the hyper-text and wider computing world. She went on to become a Professor, then Dean at Southampton, then President of the BCS, followed by President of the ACM, the New York-based global computing institution. In 2007 she formed the Web Science Trust with Sir Tim Berners-Lee and Sir Nigel Shadbolt. Her status was recognised in 2009 when she was appointed a Dame. In the mid-1990s, long after OWL, her group were responsible for a novel hypertext environment called Multi-cosm and I was appointed Non-Executive Chairman of the company which took it to market).

Back in 1987, IBM wanted us to sign a contract to develop our hypertext systems for their platform. The contract was to be with IBM Europe and was written in French and under French law. I asked our lawyers WJ Burness to recommend someone to advise on this and they suggested a lawyer, Charlie Campbell, who, although a Scot, was based in Paris and licensed in French law. Charlie was delightful; he stepped me through the IBM contract and advised me of any small issues that should concern me and that I should raise with IBM.

As a UK lawyer based in Paris, apparently, he had been intimately involved in defining the legal processes surrounding the Channel Tunnel between France and England a decade before. He asked me who I thought had legal jurisdiction should a crime be committed inside the tunnel. I guessed that it perhaps changed halfway across. "No," said Charlie. "We couldn't reach agreement on that, so there is no recognised jurisdiction in the Tunnel. It's like international waters."

So, in the middle of getting our contract with IBM sorted, I discovered that if you were to murder somebody in the middle of the Channel Tunnel there would be no fixed way of knowing which police force, if any, would prosecute you. (Much later, this odd situation led to the development of a drama series, *The Tunnel*.)

The initial training of IBM to sell Guide in France involved some 20 IBM staff, quite a commitment from IBM to such a new product at the time. One of the IBM sales school-trained salespeople, Sylvie Pelvilain, was in that team that went on to pitch Guide to several French companies. She was later persuaded to move to OWL in Edinburgh to work for Ken in international sales, and cemented her transfer to Scotland by falling for and getting married to OWL's Martin Smith.

IBM had decided to invite Renault's Pergamin to visit their PC development centre in Boca Raton, 50 miles north of Miami in Florida. This was intended to impress him of the commitment being shown by IBM. Pate and de Testa flew in from Paris and Robbie McLaren and I were to represent OWL. Robbie got there first, flying in from Edinburgh, and I was coming down from our Seattle office. We spoke on the phone, and I asked if Robbie had seen the IBM Europe guys as we were all based in the same hotel. He asked what they looked like, and I described de Testa as a Frenchman in his early 30s who usually wore a leather jacket. "You can stop there," said Robbie. "I haven't seen anybody yet in the whole State under about 70 years old."

We collectively gave Pergamin the full sales pitch and we thought it had gone well. What we didn't know was that Apple had also invited him to Cupertino to pitch Hypercard for Renault's application.

Apple had declared back in 1985 that they would no longer sell direct to corporations and that in future all sales would be via dealers. Clearly, that policy turned out to be a flexible one and Pergamin was treated like royalty, including meetings with CEO John Sculley and Hypercard developer Bill Atkinson. After all this heavyweight sales effort, it perhaps wasn't surprising that Renault decided to go with Apple rather than us..

IBM were disappointed but they decided to continue to work with us on developing a hypertext system. They even made an announcement to the press in February 1988 that they were launching a product specifically to compete with Apple's Hypercard which they called HyperDocument, based on OWL's Guide and bundled with an IBM painting/drawing program called, weirdly, 'Rasit the Owl'.

This project involved working with the PC engineers at Boca Raton. We negotiated a contract with them which involved stage payments for the design phase, the implementation phases, and a final payment to be triggered when we delivered the system to their satisfaction.

The IBM Boca Raton people had a special request: "could they make these payments to our US office in Bellevue?" If they invoiced us at our UK office, they told us, then the IBM UK operation would take a 3% handling fee for managing the transaction. We were happy to accommodate that. Money was money, as long as we received it somewhere in our company we didn't care, so we agreed that that was just fine.

A purchase order arrived at our Bellevue office but as we had failed to carefully outline the terms of our agreement with Boca Raton, they invoiced it and IBM paid it – all of it – $500,000-worth.

I was mortified!

We had yet to even supply the design phase. I phoned up my contact in IBM at Boca Raton and explained our mistake and offered to pay back the money. "Oh, for God's sake don't do that," he said. "That would be far too difficult for us to manage. Just don't mess up."

We delivered most of the system as agreed but IBM never managed to get a customer for it. Eventually they cancelled our contract, but they paid us a cancellation fee. It seemed to me that this was the first time I had met a major multinational corporation that had treated us fairly instead of trying to screw us.

Dealing with Hewlett-Packard for example, hadn't been a smooth process. HP had a habit of frequently changing personnel. On one occasion we had had a useful progress meeting with HP in California but when we flew back to the UK the next day, we received notice on our arrival home that the people that we had just met had been reassigned to another project overnight.

A few months later I was asked to join an SBDS progress meeting at Ford's headquarters in Dearborn, an upmarket suburb of Detroit. I was starting from Seattle and the only flights that worked were quite complicated: Seattle to Vancouver, Vancouver to Toronto and finally Toronto to Detroit.

When I got to Detroit in late evening my luggage had gone missing somewhere along the way. The clothes that I was standing in didn't seem appropriate for the meetings with Ford, so I drove around Detroit looking for somewhere to buy some fresh clothes. Driving around some parts of Detroit late at night, on your own, is really not recommended, but eventually I spotted an open Kmart store. My own sports jacket was OK, so I bought a pair of trousers, a shirt and a (nylon) tie, and showed up at Ford the next morning suited and booted.

Unknown to me, this particular day was Ford's monthly 'dress-down Friday' and everybody else was wandering around in jeans, sweatshirts and sneakers.

The Ford people told me in confidence about a discussion they had had with HP. The HP folks had apparently told them that they really didn't need OWL anymore, that they could easily deliver the document system without our specialist hypertext software. Luckily Ford told them they weren't interested: "when we ask OWL for things, they bust a gut to get it done, but when we ask you for anything, we just get a complex proposal accompanied by a hefty bill".

The Service Bay Diagnostic System was eventually completed and deployed by Ford. The distribution of technical manuals via CD-ROM and electronic updates worked well and they were very pleased with it.

But I was learning how to survive in the US technology world – expect everybody to try and screw you, particularly the larger corporations, and you won't be disappointed.

As Andy Grove of Intel put it: 'only the paranoid survive'.

12

BELLEVUE BLUES

Alan Boyd was superb at networking, product marketing and media relations and quickly created a huge level of visibility for our product from a standing start. However, he was much weaker in operations and administration and seemed to have an aversion to hiring anybody who was brighter than he was. Maybe he didn't want anybody who would challenge him.

His Sales Manager, John Nelson, didn't use our product, indeed he could barely switch on a computer, but Alan justified him on the strength of his telephone manner, which I had to admit was very good indeed. As many of our sales were inbound calls arising from our advertising and press coverage, a good telephone voice did seem to be important.

We had some bad luck with our choices of receptionist/personal assistant. One, a single mum with two kids, seemed to scrape by in relative poverty but despite that was frequently picked up at the end of the day by a relative in a huge limousine. One day she suddenly disappeared never to return; we learned later that her brother had just murdered her grandfather.

Then there was a smart young woman whose family ran a drug store in Los Angeles, until it was uncovered that it was a *real* drug store – her family were actually involved in the illegal narcotics business in LA. She also disappeared suddenly one day, never to return.

Another of Alan's early hires was much more successful. Dave Coffman was a techie geek whose interest in the nuts and bolts of technology was perfect for his role as tech support in our Bellevue office. He became a fixed part of the organisation and survived all the subsequent changes of management at OWL International Inc.

Alan also hired Barb Landis to head up our sales operation in the USA. Barb was an experienced ex-IBM salesperson who managed our relationships with our US opportunities.

I had decided, as a matter of policy, at the setting-up of our Seattle subsidiary, that no source code of our software would ever be sent to our US office. I had seen enough dodgy evidence of technology being copied by unauthorised transfers, or by employees taking code with them when they left for a rival, to be convinced that industrial espionage at very senior levels was rife in the American personal computer software industry.

We had been advised that patent protection was not normally available for software inventions in the UK and so we had taken the route of merely asserting our copyright and ensuring that we maintained our trade secrets. As a result, we jealously guarded the source code of all our software and none of it ever left our Edinburgh headquarters.

Another policy that we learned to adopt was to ensure that there was never much cash in OWL International Inc.'s bank account, as Alan was inclined to spend any funds that he had available. We made sure he had enough for his marketing and trade show activities, but not much more.

He was very good at networking with the industry, creating an impact, and excellent at opening new sales opportunities, but unfortunately, he wasn't particularly good at nurturing or closing them. In most cases we had to deploy some of our software engineers to move the deals towards a conclusion.

That was when I discovered the real definition of an expert: 'an individual who lives 4,000 miles away'. Whenever we shipped a Phil Cooke, Stuart Harper or Robbie McLaren to a US prospect they were received well, and the prospective customer was always impressed that a significant senior expert had come over from Europe specially to meet with them. Later I discovered the same thing applied in reverse; European prospects always found US-based staff, shipped over from the States, to be unduly impressive.

Relations with Alan began to deteriorate. He didn't meet his targets and he began to dodge attending meetings or even reporting to the main board, of which he was still the Marketing Director. We found that more and more we ended up having to cover up for his lack of performance at the board meetings.

After our excellent first year performance, the company had been increasingly missing our forecast numbers. In 1985/86 we had only achieved £257,000 against a forecast of £356,000, but in 1986/87 we were way off, achieving only £564,000 against a forecast of £1,208,000. Every year we had managed to achieve impressive growth, but it wasn't enough, and was way below our forecasts.

Naturally, our investors weren't happy with this and decided that we should have a change of Chairman. Graham Bowen had been a good supportive Chairman but, it was felt, lacked the discipline to drive us hard and keep us in line. Also, his electronics-based technology experience was so very different from ours that he really couldn't offer much in the way of useful advice as to how we were developing our opportunities in personal computer software solution markets.

Our investors and Non-Executive Directors had met

without us, and they decided that they wanted to replace Graham Bowen with David Thomson, our non-executive director from Syntech who had previously run the software house SPL.

I wasn't at all happy about this as I thought the conflict of interest between being both a key investor and Chairman was inappropriate. However, there was nothing else for it and I was forced to accept David as Chairman. Looking back, he turned out to be an excellent Chairman, was always very fair and supportive of our ambitious business activities, but also quite capable of 'pinning me up against a wall' and giving me a dressing down when he felt that was what I needed.

Our team was growing steadily and our office in the old primary school at Abbeymount Techbase was bursting at the seams. We really needed to move to accommodate our growing workforce. One of my colleagues in the local branch of the BCS worked at Brown Brothers, a subsidiary of the engineering business Vickers plc., and he told me that they had some spare office accommodation that they were looking to rent to a suitable tenant.

We agreed to move into their otherwise empty 1960s three-storey office block situated above their large heavy engineering factory in the north of Edinburgh. The factory below us was responsible for manufacturing massive stabiliser systems for large ocean-going ships and when the cranes in the roof of the factory were used to move huge pieces of equipment around the building the whole place, including the offices, would shake, giving the impression of a minor earthquake.

Originally we took the third floor and later we expanded to also occupy the second floor.

And we soon learned to take the 'earthquakes' in our stride.

∼

WHENEVER ANY OF us were over in the Bellevue office, Alan usually worked late, after which we would often end up in a local bar drinking from about 9pm until around midnight, involving large quantities of beer, whisky, nuts and, not infrequently, some Pacific Northwest oysters, which were excellent.

As we were leaving the office one night in September 1987 Alan printed out a graph which he told me plotted the value of the share options that he had been awarded while he was at Microsoft. The line in the graph ended at a value of around $7.2 million.

Alan had been employee number 31 at Microsoft, joining in 1980, the year before the PC launch. The IBM PC in 1981 powered by Microsoft's MS-DOS had completely transformed the company's fortunes, and he had been allocated share options throughout this period. Because he had been such a senior executive he had been classified by the tax authorities as an 'insider' with access to confidential information that could affect the share price, and so there were restrictions on how he could subsequently trade his shares. He was blocked from selling any of his stake until two years after his leaving date, and then he was permitted to sell up to 20% of his allocation each quarter for five quarters.

As the clock hit midnight, he looked at his watch and said, "Great. I'm now free to sell Microsoft shares." He had decided to sell his Microsoft shares as soon as he could; he didn't think Bill Gates could really succeed without him. Of course, that turned out to be a huge misjudgement. His then stake in Microsoft would have grown by a factor of around 800 and today would be worth in the billions of dollars – if he hadn't sold them.

We'd been downing beers and whiskies as usual all evening and we finally climbed into Alan's Porsche for him to drive me back to my hotel. On the way we were pulled over by a police car and the officer clearly suspected that Alan was too drunk to drive – which indeed he was.

I was wondering how I was going to get back to my hotel when, amazingly, the cop decided that Alan wasn't really too drunk, and he was allowed to get back into the car. Surprisingly, in those days US police officers didn't carry breathalysers – if they had he would surely have been taken away, and I would have been left stranded in his Porsche at the side of the freeway.

A few weeks later, on 19th October 1987, global stock markets suddenly crashed in what became known as 'Black Monday', where they experienced the largest percentage drop in history. Most US stocks, including Microsoft, lost a huge amount of their value. This meant that Alan had just lost, on paper, millions of dollars, and in the interim he had been unable to sell more than 20% of his holdings.

This, clearly, didn't go down well.

When we attended that year's Comdex in November, relations with Alan had soured and he was in a distinctly unhelpful mood. Robbie McLaren and I were there, and Alan's attitude didn't really matter to us as by then we knew how to get into the big receptions in which so much business was done. Still, Alan had not told us about that year's late-night exclusive penthouse suite party, where the movers and shakers of the industry would be hanging out. We had dinner and were walking back through the endless corridors of the Riviera resort one evening when we happened across a senior Apple executive we knew coming the other way. "Psst," he said, "follow me", and led us upstairs to the party. Alan seemed a bit nonplussed when we walked in.

Meanwhile we had been approached by Microrim, a software company in nearby Redmond who were best known for publishing a relational database called R:Base, a competitor to market leader Ashton-Tate's dBase. They expressed an interest in potentially buying our business and wanted to learn more about us. We investigated them and found that their company was estimated to be worth $40 million or so.

We met with their President, Dave Hull, and his team at their Redmond office, not far from Bellevue. Hull wasn't a technology guy; he had previously been a senior executive at the Carnation milk company and had been hired as CEO to grow their business.

The executive who was doing the detailed work, the 'diligence', on their acquisition process was William G (Bill) Nisen, who had previously headed New Business Development at Lotus Development Corporation in Boston for Mitch Kapor before heading up marketing and sales at Seymour Papert's MIT spin-off Logo Computer Systems International (LCSI) in Montreal. Bill had recently returned from the East Coast back to his native Seattle as his mother was getting infirm and needed a little more support.

We were intrigued by Microrim, which certainly seemed like a much better-managed business than our own one. We invited them over to Edinburgh to learn more about us. Hull brought a small team to visit us, and we went out one evening for a company-wide Mexican meal so that they could meet more of our staff. Unfortunately, one of our engineers got extremely drunk and decided to tell Hull what he thought of him, his company, and his attempts to buy our business. He was bundled into a taxi and out of the way, but Hull seemed to find it all very amusing.

Unknown to us at the time, they also visited Peter Brown at the University of Kent to see if they could pick up the technology cheaper from him. Peter told us about this subterfuge later.

Our meeting seemed to go well. Hull was particularly taken by a visit to Glasgow to visit the Scottish Development Agency, where he got a slick presentation on the wonders of Silicon

Glen, the SDA's attempt to brand Scotland as a high-tech location. He seemed more impressed with Glasgow, a city closer in style to North American ones, than our more ancient city of Edinburgh with its medieval centre.

We followed up with a return visit to their office in Redmond but during this meeting Hull made it abundantly clear that Microrim were looking to buy our technology as cheaply as possible, and that we weren't worth very much to him. I'm not sure what he thought he was achieving with these remarks but as soon as we heard this it didn't take us long to put an end to the discussions. We still had a pretty ambitious opinion of our future prospects, and we certainly weren't going to be sold in a fire sale.

However, Bill Nisen, who had done most of the Microrim diligence into us, was clearly impressed by what he saw of our technology, and quite unimpressed with what he saw of his management at Microrim and he left that company shortly afterwards.

Meanwhile, I got a severe ticking off from David Thomson for progressing the talks with Microrim without consulting the board. It was made very clear that I'd better not try that ever again. Fair enough; all activities which involved any change in the potential value of the business must always be shared with the shareholders.

A few weeks later, on 11 December, I got a phone call from Alan Boyd at 8.25pm UK time. He wanted to tell me that he was instructing his lawyer to sue us for $8.4 million. His claim was that we hadn't delivered his contractual entitlement to share options in Office Workstations and that he was aiming to recover his 'losses'.

There was absolutely no basis for his claim – we had delivered the option programme as agreed in his contract, and indeed no follow-up lawsuit was ever presented to us.

I immediately called David Thomson. Alan knew very well

that our balance sheet was quite poor, including several large unpaid debts incurred by him at OWL International Inc. There was no possibility of him, even if he could prove his case, getting much money – as they say 'you can't get blood from a stone'.

David and I concluded that suddenly losing millions of the paper value of his Microsoft shares may have destabilised him somewhat and it seemed that he had decided that he didn't want to continue with us at OWL. We both concluded that it seemed clear that effectively he was asking us to fire him.

We took advice from our lawyers in Edinburgh, WJ Burness, and asked them for a reference to a competent employment lawyer in Seattle. They gave us the name of Dick Prentke of Perkins Coie.

So, David Thomson and I set off for Seattle on 21st December 1987. My wife Barbara was a bit worried that heading off so close to Christmas was a risk that I might not make it back in time for the festivities.

We visited the offices of Perkins Coie, whose name was in big letters on the side of their very own skyscraper office building in downtown Seattle. I learned that among others, they were the lead counsel for Boeing, America's largest manufacturing company. Dick Prentke, we discovered, was a graduate of Princeton and Harvard Law School; we did wonder whether our tiny little business was operating way out of its league.

Prentke was reassuring: "Good news," he declared. "Washington is a 'right to work' state".' When we asked him what that meant, he said, "It means that it's easy to fire people." It wasn't difficult to calculate compensation for loss of office for Alan's notice period and as we were happy for him to retain his shares in the company – as he had undoubtedly contributed greatly in the early days to put us on the map of the US software scene – we thought it should all be cut and dried.

We had sent Alan a message that we would be coming into the office and asked that he be there for our meeting. When we met, we told him that we wanted him to step down from the company, identified a range of management failures, and told him of the conditions of his departure, that he would receive the full compensation for loss of office and that he was allowed to retain his shares.

We asked him to remove his own property, took him off as a signatory on the bank account and arranged to change the locks on the door to the office.

He didn't seem very surprised.

And we did get back to the UK in time for Christmas.

IT WASN'T JUST the management team that had lost patience with Alan, among the OWL staff I discovered that he had gained the nickname 'Nulland Void'.

After his departure we discovered that, even although he knew that we were not in great financial health, he had still managed to buy non-business-related objects, including an expensive waterbed for himself on the company's credit card.

A few months later I was an attendee at a Microsoft conference in Seattle and there was a reception afterwards at Bill Gates's house. I mentioned to Gates that we had parted company with Alan.

"Yeah," he said. "I guess we made him too rich for you," presumably referring to the fact that Alan's Microsoft shares had recently become tradeable.

By this time, I had picked up the intelligence that Microsoft had been quite comfortable when Alan left them in 2005 to join us. As their company was starting to professionalise its management, loose cannons like Alan Boyd were becoming less valued, and they had been relaxed to see him go.

Over a year later Alan Boyd's wife Ginger asked to meet with me over lunch. She was divorcing him and wanted any information I might have that would help her case. I mentioned the $7 million or so value of his Microsoft stock and her response was, "Oh, surely you don't believe that as well, do you?"

It would seem that Alan had never shared the graph showing the value of his Microsoft stock with his wife. In any case, it seemed to me that Bill Gates would be the one person who would know whether he had become substantially wealthy from his Microsoft option allocation.

And he had confirmed that he had.

13

TOPPING UP THE TANK

At the beginning of 1988, having just lost our US lead, Alan Boyd, our company was not in great shape. Although we were continuing to double our sales every year, we were still failing to achieve our forecast revenues and our losses were mounting. It was obvious that we would need to urgently raise fresh capital. I spoke with our investors and agreed a small new top-up round of investment, even though it threatened to dilute our stake in the business in the process. The sum agreed was modest at £175,000 but it would tide us over.

Over the years I had maintained a good relationship with all our investors except, unfortunately, with 3i. Although 3i had an excellent resource of technical expertise in their Solihull office in the west Midlands, these experts were only used for their due diligence and weren't available otherwise to give any help to their investee businesses. They also didn't appoint a proper Board Director, but they did have monitoring rights, and they tended to show up at board meetings from time to time.

This policy was extremely frustrating as they invariably didn't understand what we had been reporting and discussing at the board between their appearances at our meetings. It was often necessary to interrupt our normal board meeting business to provide extra explanation when they did choose to come so they could catch up. This made it slightly difficult to keep board discussions at the level of strategic issues.

They also tended to change the investment manager assigned to us fairly frequently, so when the latest manager, Roger Colwill, the fourth 3i executive in as many years allocated to our case, came to introduce himself, I had run out of patience and gave him a dusty reception. As it turned out, this wasn't very fair; it transpired he did seem to have a better understanding of early-stage technology business than his (mostly clueless) predecessors.

The rule, which I then learned the hard way, is that you must love your investors, even when they are a pain in the neck. It's not a good idea to fall out with anybody who owns a significant stake in your business. You never know when you might need their support.

In this case, the week before we were due to close this emergency investment 3i decided that they were not going to participate in this round.

This was a major blow. This could really bring down the whole company.

After all, we weren't in the best of shape at this time, although we were clearly making great progress with partners such as IBM and Hewlett-Packard and with customers such as Ford. On the other hand, our technology had not taken off as forecast, our Macintosh market had been suddenly wiped out by Hypercard, our Microsoft Windows market had hardly taken off yet, and the management of our Bellevue office was completely dysfunctional.

Fortunately, we had maintained, to some extent, the confidence of our other three investors. In the absence of 3i, the others decided that to punish 3i, the non-participant investor, the investment would be made at a low share price and the price per share was dropped back down to £1 a share – the value of our start-up equity back in 1984 – severely diluting anybody, particularly 3i, who had decided not to take part in it.

This would normally be seen as a highly negative result for the founders of the business, but I quickly realised that it also gave us a tremendous opportunity. For a relatively small amount of money, we founders could retain our share of our equity in the business. It also gave me the possibility to offer shares in the company, at effectively a start-up share price, to Professor Peter Brown. I had felt a little guilty that he had never been able to have a small equity stake in the business, so I was very glad that he was happy to invest at this time.

In negotiating this deal, I still wanted to retain the possibility of an upside, should it still be possible to deliver a good return to our shareholders, as we still hoped and expected to do. We still thought that we had good prospects – we were clearly pioneers in a field that many observers believed had huge potential.

I negotiated a deal that should we still be able to meet reasonably ambitious revenue, profit and exit price, then our investors would allow us to retain more of the value of the business. In these circumstances they would convert a proportion of their shares into worthless shares without any voting or redemption rights – what was called 'burning them' – so they would effectively no longer count as proper equity.

By this ratchet mechanism, if we could eventually sell the company for more than £6 million, the 'management' stake in the company – and therefore our share in the proceeds – would rise from about 35% to around 55%.

The investors were comfortable agreeing to this. After all, they were mostly interested in the final exit price of the busi-

ness. One which would give them a good return on their investment and simultaneously incentivise us to achieve that was in
all our interests – theirs and ours.

So, we completed our emergency investment round and
lived to fight another day.

14

NURTURING OUR AMERICAN OWL

I n the absence of Alan Boyd, my deputy Stuart Harper went over in early 1988 to run the Bellevue office and start sorting out the situation Alan had left behind. He quickly negotiated payment schedules with all the suppliers to whom we owed money.

He was helped by Bill Nisen, who had left Microrim partly because he had been disgusted at the management style of Dave Hull, including the way he had behaved towards us. Bill had agreed to help us sort things out initially on a consultancy basis, however we were quickly becoming more and more impressed with him. He seemed to understand our technology very well, seemed completely trustworthy and dependable, and he handled customer contacts well. It wasn't long before we asked him to become President of OWL International Inc.

Our sales were picking up as more and more early adopters who were also PC users were buying our software to try out the hypertext concept that Apple were helpfully spending a lot of money promoting.

Some of the applications were turning out to be good reference sites, such as a medical training course at Cornell University Hospital in New York City.

Robbie McLaren and I were invited to visit Cornell to meet with Jonathan LaPook, a consultant physician based there who was leading this project (and later became the chief medical correspondent for CBS News). He gave us a demonstration of their system which incorporated video sequences from a videodisk triggered by the various parts of a Guide hypertext document. The combination of the educational materials with the video sequences was an excellent early implementation of effective hypermedia courseware.

Back in those days the hardware to run a sophisticated multimedia application such as this one at Cornell University wasn't an easy off-the-shelf purchase. In addition to the basic personal computer, you had to install a special extra audio board and a super VGA graphics board, and then to replay moving video clips you had to install a video board made by a specialist company such as VideoLogic, along with a source of video sequences such as a LaserDisc player. Before the invention of the DVD, these videodiscs were a clumsy 30cm across. Clearly this is quite a lot of kit to deliver a multimedia experience. The equivalent today is a pocket-sized smartphone.

I was keen to create some demonstrations of how hypertext could be used effectively. I authored an interactive hypertext edition of the July 1988 edition of *Communications of the ACM*, which was a special issue devoted to hypertext developments. The ACM had requested that people in the hypertext community submit an electronic hypertext version of the issue, and all the contents were made available to us in advance. The various versions developed for different systems were then made available by the ACM and I think the interactive Guide edition was a very effective one. I was also intrigued by how traditional news might be presented and I took as a model a well-structured newspaper, *USA Today*, which had many navigation techniques to guide people through their several sections. I branded our hypertext demo edition *USA Tomorrow*.

Bill started to knock the company in Bellevue back into shape. He sacked Barb Landis, which annoyed me a little; it wasn't that she was a particularly good salesperson, but it left us suddenly without a Sales Manager. Not only that, one of our engineers from Edinburgh, John Briggs, was staying at Barb Landis's house at that time, while completing some Guide conversion work, so it also turned out to be a little bit awkward for him.

I tried to convince Bill in future to hire a new manager first before sacking the current one, but I wasn't thinking about the flexibility of the high-tech labour market in Seattle – it didn't take him very long to hire Bob Bannon as our new Sales Manager.

I was also learning more about the way sales executives work in the USA. It seemed that salespeople have a range in which they comfortably operate, so the person who can do a $100,000 deal is not the same as the person who makes $1 million deals or the person who books $10 million deals. Clearly as we grew, we needed to up our game and bring in people who operated at a higher level.

ONE DAY I arrived in the Bellevue office to be told that they were making a visit to the Boeing engineering centre a few miles away and did I want to come along?

Of course I did.

When we got down to Boeing, we were ushered into a room with about 20 engineers, every one of whom had a copy of Guide; they were experimenting with developing potential online technical publishing projects. It all looked very promising, but the aerospace industry is famously very conservative and resistant to installing innovative technology on their planes and I don't think any of those projects ever turned into any real substantial business for us.

I was discovering that we were still largely stuck in the early adopter market; the one that Bill Gates had estimated was worth 1,500 copies back in 1984. That market had grown since then, but we were still not mainstream. Our product was largely being used to experiment with the concept of hypertext but most of these didn't turn out to be real projects with substantial budgets.

Nevertheless, some of these early adopters were very useful in getting our technology more widely known. One was Halsey Minor, who used the Guide Envelope technology to publish stand-alone interactive hypertext bulletins of technology news. This turned out to be a precursor to his CNET technology news website, which he launched in 1993. It turned out to be an early successful example of an online technology news site and was eventually sold to CBS in 2008.

As the PC in the 1980s was mostly aimed at the office administration market, it was not designed to deliver multi-media (such as audio and video) material. Of course, you could add extra boards to allow audio and video processing, but that was a complex and expensive process.

We had been approached by Philips who had a new integrated multimedia system under development, called CD-i, and they asked us to build the authoring software environment for this platform. This was an ambitious project; it was effectively a forerunner to the DVD as an entertainment delivery device. It was to be launched in New York, and we were invited along to support the launch.

I flew to New York from the UK and Bill arrived late after-

noon from Seattle but his luggage had gone missing somewhere along the way. As he was to be part of a rather
prestigious product launch at 10am the next day and only stood
in his jeans and a T-shirt this would seem to be a problem, but I
hadn't reckoned on the American 'can-do' way of solving a
situation.

He phoned Bloomingdale's department store and arranged
that we would arrive there when they opened at 8.30 the next
morning, and they agreed to assemble a suit, shirt, tie and
shoes from various departments in one location for us to
quickly pick up, suitable for a product launch at a fancy New
York location. The next morning, we took an early cab to the
store, got the clothes, and made it back in plenty of time for the
10am launch. Bill even managed to get United Airlines to pay
for his new Armani suit – those being the days when airlines
seemed to take responsibility when they lost their customers'
luggage.

When we got there, we discovered that the Philips people
had spent most of the night trying to get their prototype kit to
work, and somehow they succeeded in getting it to function
sufficiently to make their launch demonstration. Their CD-i
multimedia system went on to have some limited impact but as
a multimedia platform it really didn't attract enough developers
to build product for it and couldn't compete with the new dedicated computer games consoles from Sony and Nintendo when
they were launched.

Our Sales Director, Bob Bannon, had been keen for me to
meet with a prospective client in Washington DC. His name
was Jeff Beegle and he worked for Bell Atlantic, one of the 'baby
Bells' created when AT&T had been split up by the US competition authorities. It serviced the telephony markets from New
Jersey down to Virginia. (Later, Bell Atlantic was to pioneer a
mobile phone service and changed its name to Verizon.)

It seemed clear to me during our meeting that Beegle was a

relatively junior employee without much clout in his company. I gave Bannon a ticking-off for incurring the substantial expense of getting us both to Washington DC to meet with a guy whose project I thought to be a complete waste of time.

What I didn't recognise was that although Beegle was indeed a technology 'geek' he seemed to be perceived as a smart futurist within Bell Atlantic. It seemed that he had the ear of its CEO, and on his recommendation Bell Atlantic subsequently contracted us to build a massive multi-million-dollar hypertext production system called Docusource, which they could sell under their own brand for technical publishing solutions.

I'm not sure I ever apologised properly to Bob Bannon but what I thought to be his 'dodgy lead' turned into one of our biggest-ever contracts.

It just goes to show, as they say, that you've got to be prepared to 'kiss a lot of frogs before you find your prince'.

As our Bellevue business continued to grow, it became obvious that we needed a larger office, and something a bit more professional for the increasing number of visitors that came to us. We took out a lease in a modern office block on 156th Ave SE Bellevue, just off the I-90 Freeway.

I arrived one day at the new offices and was a bit taken aback to find that the sign painted at the front door of our office stated: 'OWL International Inc. Global Corporate Headquarters'.

As our global corporate headquarters was in Edinburgh, 4,000 miles away, and OWL International Inc. was a wholly owned subsidiary, I wondered what I should do about this. OWL International was the global sales and marketing division of the company, but the strategic direction and all the engineering behind the company remained in Edinburgh.

The conclusion I came to was – do nothing.

It seemed much more important that visitors to our US office were impressed that they were meeting with senior decision-makers. We had relatively few visitors to our Edinburgh office. It made sense to allow the slight exaggeration to be sustained that our Bellevue office was indeed the global corporate headquarters. Also, Americans like to think they are at the centre of everything and there didn't seem to be much point in disabusing them of this.

Bill had hired a couple of excellent senior executives to support him. Rick Dillhoff, Chief Finance and Operating Officer managed all the operations and the finances in the business, and Jim Culbertson headed up our Marketing and Sales Operations.

Both of these were real heavyweight C-level executives; at only three years old we were beginning to become quite an effective business.

15

A BETTER GUIDE

We continued to develop the Guide product and had released Guide 2.0 in 1988 to run on Windows 2.0, which was a much more stable system than Windows 1.4. We had also developed a simple scripting language, which we called Logiix, which could execute simple programs, send messages to the serial port to drive external devices, such as videodisk players and control the layout of hypertext windows, including, with the appropriate optional graphics board, embedded video sequences on the computer screen. We also included a 'desk accessory' called Scribbler, which allowed authors to assemble graphs and charts very quickly, and then embed them into their Guide documents.

While Guide 2.0 was under development I had been asked by a customer if we could add a minor feature to the product. I had a word with our lead developer Gordon Dougan and he said it was no problem and would only take him a couple of hours. Robbie McLaren, the Product Marketing Manager of Guide, soon came charging into my office. "What do you think you are doing?" he said. I explained that Gordon had said it was a trivial addition.

"It might well be," said Robbie, "but it will also need to be tested and documented in the user manual, and then thoroughly checked. It will put the product release back by weeks."

That was when I learned my lesson. Don't ever mess with the product, especially when it has been well planned and was getting near to release. And leave it to the proper process. Luckily, Robbie knew this better than I did.

On the 23rd and 24th of May 1988 we decamped once more to an off-site strategy session, this time at Airth Castle near Stirling, where we decided to focus our efforts on custom engineering of hypertext solutions for the kind of large projects that were being brought to us. In particular, our US operation had concentrated on our retail offering, but at this event we made the strategic decision to set up a custom engineering function in our US office, led by Brain Newton, one of our best software engineers, who then transferred from Edinburgh to Bellevue.

Christian Raby, the CEO of Frame, a French software distributor who handled the distribution in France of several major PC software packages, showed an interest in Guide. He was keen that we localise Guide for the French market and when that was completed, he invited me to join him at the grand old George V Hotel off the Champs-Élysées in Paris for his Guide product launch in France. It was, he explained, his 'lucky' hotel for product launches.

I had also been contacted by Neil van der Merde, the CEO of Xcel, a South African software distributor. He wanted to visit us in our Edinburgh office and initially I wasn't very welcoming as I had a pretty negative attitude to South Africa at the time. This was 1988 and apartheid was still in force – Nelson Mandela wouldn't be elected President for another six years.

Later, I got to know Neil and his company much better when I made my first visit to South Africa, arriving the day after the country's referendum to change the constitution which would put an end to apartheid. There was excitement in the air as the results were counted – even although only whites had been allowed to vote, the majority in favour of changing the constitution turned out to be substantial.

I discovered that for years Neil had actively pursued a policy of employing and promoting black executives. Also, it turned out that his wife was a medical doctor who had chosen to give up her lucrative work at a private, mostly white, hospital, to work in a public hospital where most of the patients were poor and black. She said she could no longer put up with handling the first-world problems of coughs and colds from her private patients and chose instead to save lives.

We had also been contacted by Masuo Yoshimoto, who ran MP Technology Inc. (MPT), a small software company based in Tokyo that was interested in the development of a version of Guide 2.0 for the Japanese market. It was to be in kanji (the Japanese writing system), and to run on their BTRON operating system – part of a Japanese government-supported technology research initiative. As a result, Gordon Dougan was dispatched to Tokyo in July 1988 to undertake a feasibility study and he returned there in October to start the development work, being joined by Callum Sword that December.

The background to this project was a bit unclear to us but it emerged that there was support for this advanced research project from the Japanese government in association with MCI, a subsidiary of the giant Matsushita electronics company (better known by its brand name, Panasonic). One of the first people to show up in the MPT office was a Matsushita engineering manager, Nobuyoshi Yokobori, who had been a student along with Masuo at their university course. They continued to be regular drinking buddies and Gordon was often (somewhat reluctantly) included in these evening drinking sessions. We Scots weren't used to the 'after-hours' drinking culture of the Japanese, but over the next months we all had to get used to it.

By November 1988, it was beginning to look like Gordon was going to be living in a tiny Japanese hotel room for months and he was feeling rather alienated in a strange city with little contact – email systems were still in the future, and phone calls were expensive. Stuart Harper remembers being phoned by Gordon pleading to be allowed to come home, but to no avail, it was a strategic project, and a well-paying one. Sorry Gordon.

Masuo Yoshimoto wasn't prepared to translate the BTRON manuals into English, so Gordon found he had to struggle with them in a mixture of C and katakana and bothering folk in the MPT office. The BTRON project was a full-blown port of our Guide system, to a very different operating system. It certainly wasn't a case of just adapting the Windows version of Guide to kanji.

Masuo was eventually persuaded to rent a couple of studio apartments for Gordon and Callum, two train journeys away from the office – a normal commute for Japanese workers. Callum was unfortunate enough to be in Tokyo in January 1989 when Emperor Hirohito died, and everything closed for a while. Fortunately, Gordon had come home for New Year and managed to postpone his return until things had returned to normal.

While Gordon and Callum were there, they did manage to find time to see the sights of Tokyo, Kyoto and Nara, and Gordon usually arranged meetings in Matsushita's office in Osaka for a Friday or Monday so they could spend the weekend in Kyoto, or do some hill-walking in the foothills between Tokyo and Mount Fuji.

Masuo insisted that his company, MPT, needed exclusive rights for Japan to the localised version of Guide 2.0 for the PC ('Kanji Guide') to make it work commercially for him. We had always had a policy of never granting exclusive rights to anybody for anything so initially we refused. However, he persuaded us that he was intending to make a significant investment on the localisation of our manuals and packaging and that he really needed to have exclusivity protection to ensure that he could hope to recoup the outlay.

We thought about it and concluded that Japan was a very difficult market to enter from the West, that you really needed to have good local knowledge and relationships which, other than Masuo, we certainly didn't and couldn't easily acquire, and so in this unique situation we decided that we were reluctantly willing to grant them exclusivity.

However, as part of this exclusivity agreement we put very high revenue targets on the deal. MPT had to book an extraordinarily high level of business over the next three years to retain their exclusivity, and if they didn't achieve these targets, we would be free to take back our product and assign it to another distributor.

Frankly, if MPT had achieved that level of business we would have been delighted. This was our first and only exclusive deal and we weren't particularly worried about it given the special situation of the Japanese market.

Of course, we didn't suspect that we were going to be approached to sell our company to a Japanese multinational corporation.

I CAME BACK from an overseas trip one Monday morning to find Terry O'Brien, our Finance Director, telling me, excitedly, that he had arranged for us to have a royal visitor to our offices: the Duke of Kent was to come to look around.

This seemed to me to be a complete waste of time and I then made it clear to everybody in the company that if anybody ever agreed to a royal visit again it would be an immediate sackable offence.

I learned later that the Scottish Hunt Ball was being held in Edinburgh that evening and that the Duke may well have been using our visit as part of the justification for the expense of his travel to his social event that night in Edinburgh.

Our Chairman, David Thomson, insisted on flying up specially from London, and he and the Lord Provost of Edinburgh made up the welcome party downstairs at the front door of the building. David was a slim and fit individual, but the Lord Provost at that time was a small, overweight woman, and a heavy smoker.

The Duke of Kent was tall and fit, and started to bound up the staircase to our third-floor office, followed closely by David Thomson and – less closely – the Lord Provost. By the time they arrived, she was ready to breathe her last.

And, as I had predicted, the whole visit turned out to be a complete waste of time.

LATER I ORGANISED A MORE appropriate visit. Ted Nelson had agreed to visit our Edinburgh office – for those of us in the hypertext community he was much more like royalty. As mentioned in Chapter 6, Ted had originally coined the term 'hypertext' in 1963 and had written *Literary Machines* to further define the concept in 1980. We had even created and published a Guide hypertext edition of *Literary Machines* and he had been impressed by our version.

During his visit, Ted and I spent some time discussing our plans and listening to his. I demonstrated to him what we were then working on in our Guide hypertext system and we discussed the issues that we were confronting at that time, mostly concerning our engineering developments regarding the management of very large volumes of documentation, including our decision to apply a variant of Standard Generalised Markup Language (SGML) with extra markup instruction to describe hypertext actions as a means of authoring huge collections of connected document sets.

We then had a session where Ted gave a presentation to all our staff and took a Q&A with our very engaged team. It was a memorable day.

In his own work, Ted was particularly concerned by the implications of recognising copyright rights within documents and devising a micropayments scheme which could handle the economics of references to valuable published material where a small payment might be appropriate.

If these matters had been properly considered when the World Wide Web was designed we would have a dramatically different media landscape from what we have today, where publishing companies – content providers who spend huge resources employing journalists, creative writers, dramatists, musicians, performers and artists to create valuable intellectual material – are starved of income while Google, Facebook and other social media sites collect most of the digital advertising revenue arising from the viewing of that content, without paying anything for its creation.

Ted never managed to create a working version of his Xanadu project even with the efforts of researchers at Brown University. His project did attract the personal support of John Walker, the founder of Autodesk, and the Xanadu development was based at the Autodesk software company from 1983 onwards, but after millions of dollars had been invested, Autodesk finally gave up and divested the project in 1992.

And then of course, in the face of the spectacular rise of the World Wide Web during the 1990s, the more complex Xanadu project never managed to prosper, and it withered. By contrast, the World Wide Web benefited from being extremely simple, and it was that basic simplicity that led to its success – it was very easy to adopt for a variety of tasks.

ONE OF THE policies that I applied at OWL was that we tried to keep our overheads under control, whether it was by using second-hand desks or keeping salary levels on a tight rein. At the Scottish Software House Federation we had instituted salary surveys which researched the level of salaries of various grades of software development staff paid in Central Scotland and we tended to pay a little below these levels. Our company was such an exciting place to work, and we were doing such interesting developments, that we didn't need to overpay. We did, however, ensure that all staff were issued with share options in the company so that they all had an interest in our growth and eventual valuation, whether by a listing or an exit.

When we finally made a profit in 1989 we declared a bonus; everybody, from the CEO (me) to the receptionist, was awarded the same bonus – £750 each. It never occurred to me that this was unusual.

The OWL Edinburgh team in 1987

IT SEEMS we were a happy family. In the period between our company formation in June 1984 and the end of 1989 we had only ever had two members of staff resign from the UK company, which in retrospect was an extraordinary achievement. One of those two emigrated to New Zealand for family reasons. The other was Lynda Hardman, who left but later returned to the fold.

The British Computer Society (BCS), the UK-based institution for computer professionals, runs an annual awards competition, the BCS Awards, for the best computing development in the UK each year, and we decided to submit the Guide hypertext system along with Professor Peter Brown at the University of Kent. The judging panel came to our office one day for a demonstration and they seemed impressed by what they saw.

Sometime later we were declared the winners of the BCS Award for 1988 and I was invited to demonstrate our system at a grand awards ceremony held at the prestigious Royal Society building at Carlton House Terrace in London. The ceremony was hosted by the then President of the BCS, Brian Oakley, the same individual who had headed up the Alvey Programme intended to encourage innovation in the UK's software scene. It was notable that we had pulled out of our Alvey consortium because our proposed innovation wasn't being recognised. Surely our BCS Award was a clear indication that the Alvey Programme, at least in this case, had failed to achieve its goals.

I demonstrated some training and technical manual implementations but the sequence that made most impact was a hypertext mock-up of a car magazine where, at a click of the mouse, the images embedded in the magazine page came to life and turned into exciting moving sequences of video with a sports car driving down a winding mountain track

On the back of this, the BBC Interactive Television Unit commissioned us to build some new interactive multimedia projects based on our hypertext technology, but this turned out to be a nightmare of a project. The BBC executives didn't really know quite what they wanted but it didn't stop them having a lofty opinion of themselves. If I was being generous, I would accept that they were mostly used to working with TV production companies, where you can continue to tweak a production even after it is has been mostly completed, until you get it right, so their attempts at accurately specifying the project in advance fell far short of what we needed.

Unfortunately, complex computer software projects can't be done that way – you really must get the specification right before you start the development. After failing to get the BBC to properly specify the project, we decided that we would write a detailed specification of what we thought they needed and encouraged them into approving it.

Once we built the system to that specification, the BBC decided that it didn't meet their needs after all and disputed paying for it. We should probably have walked away from the job once it became clear that we didn't have a meeting of minds about what they needed. All of this was complicated by what seemed to me to be the huge sense of entitlement evidenced by the behaviour of the BBC folk.

Because they were paid for by the public through the licence fee, and were not a commercial business, they seemed to have the attitude that they were the righteous party in all situations. We had successfully completed similar projects for customers all over the world, but the BBC turned out to be one of our least happy customers. Even so, they did pay us in the end.

16

GUIDEX – INDUSTRIAL-STRENGTH HYPERTEXT

One of the most frequently raised criticisms of Guide was that, as a stand-alone authoring platform, it was fine for small documents or document sets, but for larger collections of documentation, authoring each hypertext button by hand was a tedious and potentially error-prone task.

In order to deal with this issue we started to develop a new 'industrial-strength' hypertext environment which we called Guidex, for people who had to deal with very large volumes of material, a market which we could see was beginning to emerge.

The development of Guidex had been driven by Phil Cooke and Ian Williams. Phil had been one of the most talented software design architects at ICL and joined us soon after we started the company. He had become the leading strategic expert in building our hypertext architecture. Ian Williams had joined us later with substantial previous experience in publishing technologies. Between them they developed an architecture that could be applied to huge collections of hypertext document sets.

We were also very aware of the problem of getting 'lost in

hypertext', where readers can find it difficult to navigate a complex hypertext system, and we wanted to develop a set of indexing and navigation tools to try and resolve some of those problems.

Initially, our sales operation in Bellevue didn't show much interest in any of this – none of their current customers were yet asking for industrial-strength hypertext authoring – but this attitude changed quite quickly when they began to unearth heavyweight documentation opportunities such as at Bell Atlantic.

In April 1988 we launched the first version of Guidex, our large-volume interactive online document management system. Core to all this was our adoption of a mark-up language called Hypertext Markup Language (HML). Tim Berners-Lee had a similar idea when he developed HTML (Hyper Text Mark-up Language), a variant of SGML which defines the underlying structure behind all World Wide Web documents.

All documents in Guidex had an associated user-defined document type, which could be any convenient system of clas-sification, descriptions such as: 'design standard', 'specification', 'production tool drawing', 'operation flow chart', 'parts list' and so on.

Such document types could determine a variety of attrib-utes, including how a document was indexed and how it was styled in the screen display or how it would appear if printed (e.g. font, style and size of type used for each level of heading, caption, footnote, etc.). The document manager automatically created a directory for each type and held its associated style files.

Every document authored in Guidex also had an attached 'catalog card' which defined title, author, date, version number, and so on, and which could be extended to include additional navigation concepts such as searchable keywords and comments. The authoring environment would first create documents in 'draft' mode until it was completed and approved, at which time its status would become 'published'.

The Guidex product was targeted at those with a need to create very large quantities of documentation; this was a totally different market from our normal Guide product, which was aimed at creating simple hypertext documents. Reflecting this complexity and powerful features, Guidex had a list price of $10,000.

We also built a set of conversion tools to help users import very large quantities of existing documents into our system, and we licensed a technology called FastTAG from Avalance Development Corporation which helped users to automatically generate a first draft of HML marked-up documents from a wide variety of sources, even from those scanned in from paper originals. It then made a first attempt to mark them up based on their appearance and implied structure.

This technology was chosen by the University of Central Florida to build a system for NASA and the Kennedy Space Centre to support operations in the Orbiter Processing Facility, to allow shuttle technicians to retrieve information and video sequences providing instructions, guidance and reference information.

We had also won a major project with a Scottish nuclear power plant, one of the very few projects we had ever won in our native Scotland. The printed Station Operating Instructions (SOI) of their mandatory manuals occupied many metres of physical shelf space and because access to these manuals was so time-critical there were 20 copies of these document sets kept at various locations around the plant.

We used our Guidex system to automate the creation of an online version of their SOIs which could be accessed at a computer anywhere throughout the building, and unlike the printed version, updates only had to be made once and were then automatically up to date at every computer point.

We also documented a production methodology for the creation of these heavyweight document collections which we called 'CAPD-M'. It consisted of several distinct stages: Capture, Author, Publish and Distribute, with a Management layer controlling the whole process.

The first stage in the process – the Capture phase – involved acquiring the source material, which was usually already available in some existing document format or, at a pinch, could be scanned in from a printed copy. This could normally be quickly converted into a suitable basic HML marked-up format using FastTAG.

The next stage – Author – was where the individual editor added value to the documents or created new material, including inserting navigational links and adding content which cannot easily be represented on static document formats such as complex diagrams, animations, or video or audio sequences.

The third stage – Publish – let users publish a collection of documents, defining the user interface and the layout style of the document collection.

The final stage – Distribute – let authors provide readers with the capability to select and display documents, and to integrate other content, such as multimedia files.

All this process was overlaid by a supervisory function – Manage – which let the responsible manager control the whole process, including support for various storage devices, building libraries – organised collections of material – recording and maintaining document characteristics and changing document status, including setting access levels where appropriate for various users.

We were now capable of delivering huge sets of interactive documents in real heavyweight industrial situations, where the efficiency of electronic delivery, either via CD-ROMs or via access to shared file systems over networks, provided real benefits compared to traditional methods. We could ensure that everyone accessed versions of documents that were always up-to-date, and we could also provide control over who had the right to access which documents.

We went on to develop a huge Guidex system to deliver operational manuals for the North Sea operations of Shell Exploration, and it also became the basis of our major Docu-source project at Bell Atlantic.

ANOTHER HEAVYWEIGHT PUBLISHING project came from an unusual source. We had been contacted by Jon Boring, a systems engineer who worked for the Dallas Theological Seminary.

He had been working on a massively ambitious plan to build the ultimate Bible study resource to be distributed on a CD. His project was to be called CD-Word and was to contain online versions of 16 volumes (two complete Greek texts, four English Bible texts, two full dictionaries, three Greek lexicons, three leading Bible commentaries, plus complete parsing for every Greek word and hundreds of detailed Bible maps, charts, illustrations and graphics).

What he had envisioned would represent a huge development project which would require us to invent all kinds of new technology: combining search navigation with hypertext navigation; multilingual presentation including in Greek and Hebrew alphabets, and mapping between key words in different languages.

Unlike many commercial projects where we often managed to extract 'pilot' or 'prototyping' fees of a few tens of thousand dollars, the Dallas Theological Seminary it seems had plenty of money to spend on this, very real, project.

I flew down to Dallas to follow up on this, picked up a

rental car and drove into the city to get to my hotel in preparation for my meetings the next morning. As I was driving along,
I had the weird impression that I was in an area that I knew,
even though I had never visited Dallas before. It was Dealey
Plaza where I began to realise that I recognised the flyover, the
grassy knoll, the picket fence and the red brick building from
which Lee Harvey Oswald had assassinated President Kennedy
in November 1963. Unlike the rest of Dallas, which has been
substantially redeveloped, the Dealey Plaza area had been
preserved, and it was as I remembered it from the news
coverage of the time.

This CD-Word project was looking to be one of the biggest
and most ambitious that we had ever undertaken, but having
established that the Dallas Theological Seminary were very
serious about what they wanted to achieve, we decided that Bill
Nisen would join me from Seattle to agree the outline of the
work.

The CD-Word project built on the Guidex developments
and funded the invention of very powerful new tools. This was
a massive project in which Dave MacLaren delivered
extraordinary feats of software engineering, including
displaying and searching Classical Greek texts. Although this
was a Bible study tool and not, on the face of it, a heavyweight
engineering project, it required much more technology than
any technical publishing project that we had ever done before.
It was also the first time ever that hypertext browsing had been
combined with full-text search – two quite distinct navigation
techniques.

The Dallas Theological Seminary had appointed Steve
DeRose to act as an external consultant to this project. His
work with hypermedia systems had begun with FRESS at
Brown University in 1979, and in 1989 he co-founded Electronic
Book Technologies and designed DynaText, the first SGML
publishing tool. This relationship with DeRose also led to

useful contacts with the Text Encoding Initiative, which all eventually fed into the development of an SGML variant called XML, a pivotal Web standard later adopted by the W3C (the World Wide Web Consortium headed by Tim Berners-Lee). This, and an interface to the Document Object Model – which defined the basic structure of documents – was significantly ahead of anything anybody else was achieving in this field at that time.

With CD-Word, the user was able to open, side by side, various Bibles in English or Greek. When the user scrolled through one document, the others would scroll in step, and clicking on a Greek word would highlight the equivalent English word and vice versa; dictionaries and commentaries could be accessed at the click of the mouse. The user could also develop their personal concordance and use the system to undertake detailed theological research or efficiently create their sermons, reports or lectures. It was the ultimate theological research tool, to be used by pastors, academic researchers, and theology students.

By this stage we had developed and matured considerably as a company since the launch of our original stand-alone Guide hypertext authoring product for the Apple Macintosh back in 1986; that had been aimed at the individual author creating relatively simple interactive documents – the equivalent of a word processor.

We were now marketing a major new system designed to deliver massive collections of online documentation for professional use in real industrial situations where the documents had to really work for a living.

Our original plan when we started our business was to develop such a system for the creation of very large collections of technical manuals and we had finally got there. Our delivery vehicle was revolutionary in that we had bypassed paper-based manuals by making the manuals viewable, and navigable, online and via a screen, as well as easily updated and interactive.

However, one of the features in our HML mark-up language was that it also allowed users to define the features (fonts, layout etc.) of the printed version of these documents should they also be desired. As a result, we also supported the creation of large printed volumes of manuals.

In October 1989, we hired the renowned marketing consultancy, Regis McKenna, to investigate the market opportunities for Guidex. Their conclusion was that there was a considerable opportunity with users who had very large documentation needs, but that we still had a huge job in that we needed to put a lot of effort into educating potential users of the value of hypertext solutions.

17

OSAKA CALLING

I n mid-August 1988 I took a phone call from the London office of Yamaichi, a Japanese corporate finance company. They wanted to speak to me about the possibility of an investment in our company from Matsushita Electrical Industrial (MEI), which sold products under the Panasonic brand, and which was the largest consumer electronics company in the world.

We had been indirectly engaged with Matsushita as they were a participant in the project we were working on with MPT in Tokyo, but at that time we had had no direct dealings with them.

As I had previously got into so much trouble with our unauthorised Microrim discussions, this time I immediately called our Chairman, David Thomson, and reported the approach. He suggested that it would be best if Yamaichi's initial meeting was held with him.

However, on Friday, 26th August, I took a call from two British Yamaichi executives who said that they 'happened' to be in Edinburgh for other business and could they 'pop in' for a

chat. They were Roderick Seligman and Simon Howell –
Seligman was supposed to be the financial lead and Howell the
technology guy, although neither impressed me with much
understanding of software businesses.

Under the circumstances I agreed to meet them and gave
them a demonstration of Guide but as they had been sprung on
me uninvited, I kept what I told them only to things that were
already in the public domain. I didn't discuss any financial
information or business performance and said that they would
have to start these discussions with my Chairman. I didn't want
to give them any information that they could later use against
us when we came to discuss the details of any investment.

There followed a series of contacts with David Thomson,
including agreeing on a confidentiality agreement between us
and Matsushita, following which we then shared with them
some of our business information. By December we received an
outline of what they thought might be a suitable relationship
between our companies.

Matsushita proposed to take an equity stake in OWL of
between 25% and 51% and to collaborate with us, on a commercial basis, on various Matsushita software projects. They also
wanted to second some of their engineers to us to work with us
and gain skills in our type of software development.

We arranged the first face-to-face meeting at our Edinburgh
office for the 9th and 10th of February 1989. The MEI representatives were Tooru Tamura and Nobuyoshi Yokobori, both
senior managers in the R&D division, accompanied by their
Yamaichi advisors.

David Thomson came up to Edinburgh for this meeting
and he opened by informing our Japanese guests that this
session had been so important to our Managing Director – me
– that I had specially arranged to have my daughter born the
day before, so it didn't interfere in any way with our
discussions.

I'm not sure whether they believed that or not, but of course it wasn't true. My wife Barbara had given birth to my daughter Claire the previous day, and Barbara had indeed been induced early – but due to concerns about her high blood pressure, and nothing to do with my work commitments.

It soon emerged that Nobuyoshi Yokobori, the manager of the R&D centre, was the driving force behind the interest in OWL. Japanese companies tend to plan for the long term and make strategic plans over decades into the future, and Matsushita had apparently concluded that they were facing a critical shortage of software development skills as consumer electronics products became more and more controlled by embedded computer chips and driven by software. They were, of course, experts in developing electronic consumer products but at that stage they didn't have deep skills in complex software development.

Also, as the leader in consumer entertainment devices, Matsushita undoubtedly thought they also needed to particularly develop skills in interactive information technology, hence their particular interest in us. No doubt they had also noticed our contribution to providing the authoring software for the Philips CD-i system (see Chapter 13), which was exactly the kind of product that Panasonic would also be expected to bring to market.

They were developing programmes with a number of Japanese universities to ensure access to better software skills, but they also thought they needed relationships with innovative commercial Western technology companies to give their software development strategy a boost.

They asked lots of questions about us – our resources, customers, technology, competition, market opportunity and so on.

David Thomson said that we couldn't contemplate selling 25% to 51% of our business because it would effectively preclude anybody else buying OWL. As a venture capital-backed business, our long-term goal was to create a valuable company and ultimately provide an exit for our investors, and this would most likely be achieved by a trade sale to an acquiring company. If we were to take a significant investment from a global multinational corporation such as Matsushita it might well block the possibility that anybody else would show an interest in buying us. Matsushita would always be able to trump any offer made.

If they wanted a close relationship with OWL, said David, they would have to buy 100% of the company.

He also stated that we were still an early-stage business with a very exciting future, so we couldn't really value the company on the basis of our current business performance. Our potential was much higher than that.

He said that he thought a fair price for OWL would be £8 million, plus a commitment from MEI to invest a further £2 million over the next two years. He quoted some recent examples of comparable trade sales of early-stage technology companies that were also not yet profitable, including Computer Pictures for $14.5 million, and Forethought for $20 million.

At this point I was glad that I hadn't got involved in such a discussion at my earlier Yamaichi meeting. David Thomson was so much more experienced than me in this area. We had had only one experience of a potential trade sale – to MicroRim – but David Thomson had had many, and his skill in negotiating technology transactions proved invaluable here.

Tamura and Yokobori said that they were mere engineers from the R&D division and were not there to negotiate the terms of any deal; that kind of discussion would be handled at a later stage when commercial managers got involved. Their job for now was to see if OWL was a good technical fit for MEI.

However, David Thomson had expertly placed an expected price on the table, and it was clearly now down on the record.

Yamaichi, as MEI's Corporate Finance advisors, really should have anticipated this and been prepared to counter our expectations of price at this stage, but as it turned out they were completely useless. Roderick Seligman was a posh boy who had been educated at Harrow, one of the UK's most exclusive private boarding schools, and frankly, he wasn't very competent as a corporate finance advisor. We were beginning to discover as the relationship progressed that he was not only poor at his job, but he was also sometimes haphazard and unpredictable in his behaviour, which often threatened to affect the orderly progress of the deal.

We didn't ourselves appoint a corporate finance advisor – we relied on our own resources led by David Thomson. MEI hadn't bought a Western company for a very long time – 15 years previously they had bought Quasar, an American TV brand, but that had been generally regarded as a very poor deal – so they were neither well versed nor comfortable in this type of situation. They initially relied on Yamaichi to advise them, which turned out to be a poor choice.

Stuart Harper and I, along with Roderick Seligman of Yamaichi, were invited to visit MEI's headquarters in Osaka and we arrived on Saturday, 20th May, leaving us the Sunday to relax before our meetings on Monday and Tuesday.

MEI's R&D headquarters were a low-rise group of buildings set around a large roundabout, in which had been erected a dozen statues of famous scientists and engineers. Looking at this group, which included Newton and Einstein, there were a few Japanese and Chinese pioneers of whom I had no knowledge. I did note though that there was one key figure that it seemed to me that was missing from this iconic group – James Clerk Maxwell – the Scottish physicist who was first to unite electricity, magnetism and light into one phenomenon, a single set of equations which described the laws of electromagnetism.

This breakthrough was so fundamental to pretty much everything that was manufactured and sold by Matsushita, I was amazed at the blank looks I got when I pointed this out. Had they really never heard of 'Maxwell's equations'?

As we entered MEI's headquarters on the Monday morning a group of workers were enthusiastically doing their morning 'jumping jack' callisthenic exercises in the fresh air at the front of the building, one of many examples which demonstrated the different workplace culture in Japan.

We started our session with a visit to the Matsushita in-house technology museum, which told the tale of the founder of the company, Konosuke Matsushita, who had been born in 1894. He had been a hugely impressive character who, despite suffering from poor health as a child, had gone on to build the largest consumer electronics business and one of the top manufacturing companies in the world.

He had managed to survive and prosper during, and then after, the Second World War, where even though he'd devoted his considerable manufacturing skills towards heavily supporting the manufacture of military equipment and ordnance for the Japanese government, had somehow succeeded in peacetime in smoothly switching his operations to becoming a dominant player in the emerging market for consumer electronics. Although he was known across Japan as 'the god of manufacturing' it seemed to me that his real achievement was in building a highly effective international sales operation. Panasonic, after all, was a leading brand known all over the world.

Long retired from the business, Konosuke Matsushita had died the month before our visit, in April 1989, at the age of 94.

The most impressive exhibit in the Museum of Technology

for me was high-definition television – this was the first time that I experienced that level of image quality – quality that has since become the standard for TV production and broadcasting although it took another 20 years or so to be widely adopted. Indeed, HD television has now been superseded by an even higher-resolution standard – 4K. Back in 1989 however, the demonstration of HD was very impressive.

We spent that afternoon outlining our technology and strategy to our hosts and had a meeting with an Executive Vice-President of Matsushita, Mr Hirata. The following day we were presented with MEI's plans for us, how they expected to make use of our skills and manage the relationship. All these meetings seemed to go well.

We were taken to dinner and afterwards Nobuyoshi Yokobori was keen to show us some typical Japanese evening activities. He took us first to a pachinko parlour which was clearly a very popular pastime judging from the rows of players sitting at the pin-ball machines; most of the players were also smoking heavily, creating a haze of tobacco smoke that completely covered the room in a choking fug.

I started with a plastic tub full of ball bearings and poured them into the hopper. After some time the lights flashed off briefly and it was clear that the parlour was closing for the night. I seemed to be winning and when we left, I went to the desk with my tubs of balls and was rewarded with my 'prize' in exchange – a comb and a toothbrush.

I was a bit puzzled by this, but Noboyoshi explained that we had to look for a nearby window painted in the same colour scheme as the pachinko parlour.

We knocked on this window and it slid up a little – I pushed my comb and toothbrush through the slot and was rewarded by some yen coming back in the opposite direction. Clearly, public gambling for cash had to be disguised in Japan.

Noboyoshi then took us to a nearby building where we travelled up in a lift to a small private apartment which served as a
bar offering liquor and karaoke and not much else.

We had a whisky each and tried a song. So this was what
passed for Japanese bonding behaviour. Still, I suppose we
were getting to know each other better.

On the next morning we got down to business: discussing
the terms of a possible acquisition. The MEI representatives
said they were happy to buy the shares from, and say goodbye
to, our venture capital investors but they had a bit of a problem
with buying the shares owned by us, the founders of the
company. They were concerned that once we had been paid for
our shares, we would lose motivation and not drive our business as aggressively as we had done in the past.

I said that there was a fundamental principle involved, and
that was that all the shareholders in the company, investors and
founders, must receive the same rewards for their shares. We
had built a company which we had fully expected would be
sold in a trade sale, and we therefore expected to realise the
return on our investment at the point when the company was
sold; it was simply not acceptable to try to treat us differently
from the other shareholders. The ongoing motivation for us as
managers in the continuing business was a separate issue
which could be solved by other incentives.

They said they understood this, but they were still unhappy
about buying all our shares at the point of acquisition. Once
again, Yamaichi weren't much use here; we would have
expected them to have given MEI some advice with such
matters, but MEI didn't seem to use them much.

MEI then summarised their current negotiation position.
Although Matsushita had that very day announced excellent
results, including confirmation that they had $7 billion in cash
on their balance sheet, they maintained that they are still very
careful investors and were determined to take a strictly

commercial line. OWL was not a very mature company, and they thought the £10–£12 million that had been suggested was far too high. They said they thought a fair value would be £4–£5 million, which would include the new investment of £2 million into the business.

They suggested that another approach be considered; they proposed that we founders should retain our shares and at some later date seek to become listed as a public company, at which point we might achieve excellent returns, but that if a listing did not turn out to be possible they would agree to ultimately buy our shares under an agreed formula.

We said that, as we had previously explained, we were not there to negotiate a deal but would report their position to our Chairman. We could, however, state without much difficulty that we believed their current proposal was quite unacceptable.

I asked them if they had discussed this with Yamaichi and they surprised us by saying they hadn't. We withdrew for a while so they could consult them.

For the rest of that day, it seemed as if there was a lot of backtracking on this 'offer'. Roderick Seligman told us that it seemed to him the offer had been withdrawn, but no one from MEI said as much to us.

We returned to the UK, and I sent a detailed note of the meeting to David Thomson. This resulted in a brief letter from him to Mr Kosaka. He wrote that there were a variety of ways of retaining our motivation after acquisition, including a 'golden hello' payment or perhaps an element of deferral in the purchase of our shares.

He then tackled the fundamental issue of our valuation. He said that we had always stated that we had set our valuation at £10–£12 million, and if they were unwilling to progress a deal on that basis, he would prefer to end the discussions there and then.

Mr Kosaka replied immediately, saying they were still

enthusiastic about a relationship with OWL, and that we should continue discussions. They suggested a key meeting in London in late June during which we would hopefully finally come to agreement on a deal.

18

A DEAL IS DONE

The crunch meeting to agree a deal was to be held in London at the end of June at the offices of Lovell White Durrant in the Holborn area of London. Lovell White Durrant were the corporate lawyers who had been retained by MEI to consummate the deal. It seemed the proposed price had returned to £8 million plus £2 million investment so on that basis we were happy to resume discussions.

MEI said that, as previously outlined, they were happy to buy institutional shares from our venture capitalists and any staff share options immediately, but they would like to defer the payment to the ongoing founder management. I said that in principle I was not particularly concerned about this, we were committed to making our relationship with MEI a success and we were looking forward to working together.

Given that Matsushita were the largest consumer electronics company in the world we all thought there could be an exciting future for us once we were part of it, given their ability to globally market new products. In retrospect it seemed we were 'wearing rose-tinted spectacles'.

They proposed buying 10% of our shares immediately, then 45% in three years and the final 45% in five years' time.

I responded that in principle that could be acceptable, but the purchase price of the deferred payments would have to be adjusted to take account of the change in value that would undoubtedly happen over that time. The fundamental principle from which I was not going to deviate was that all shareholders must receive the same effective return for their shares, so the price of the deferred shares must be adjusted in some way if they were to be delayed by three and five years.

I suggested that the final price paid needed to take account of either the rate of bank interest over the period, or alternatively could be adjusted in line with the UK government's published rate of inflation.

I assumed this was a perfectly sensible approach that everyone would easily understand, but it seemed to create a huge problem for MEI. Bank interest rates and inflation rates in Japan have traditionally been very low, and initially they did not seem to understand the basis of our problem. Unfortunately, here in the UK, especially at that time, a payment of £5 in 1990 was worth significantly more than a payment of £5 in 1995, and we needed that difference to be resolved.

We hosted the MEI team at dinner that evening. David Thomson had managed to book something special, Rules in Covent Garden. First opened in 1798, it was the oldest restaurant in London, and the Japanese were suitably impressed by the meal, the wine and the unique setting.

It took much longer than I had expected to agree on the terms of our deferred payment. I suspect they had been authorised to pay up to the £8m and not a penny more, and this request for an adjustment for the delayed shares had caused a problem back in Osaka that needed to be resolved at a senior level. Eventually we reached agreement that our deferred payment should be adjusted to take account of the UK government's retail price index over the three- and five-year periods. Eventually, on 28[th]June, we finally agreed the outline terms with MEI.

We then needed a private discussion with David Thomson about the position of our negotiated ratchet. The terms of the ratchet had two components – a performance element, in which we had to achieve various levels of profitability over time, and an exit price more than £6 million. Although we hadn't achieved the performance element, we had comfortably exceeded the target exit price.

I suggested to David that our investors were fundamentally interested in the return on their investment and as we had more than achieved that, the ratchet should trigger. He seemed initially reluctant to accept that and insisted that we needed to achieve the performance as had been defined.

Eventually he turned to my partner, Stuart Harper, who was also in the room, 'What do you think?' he asked. Stuart said that our exit target had been £6 million, but that we had achieved £8 million, and that the investors should be very happy with that return and the ratchet should absolutely trigger.

At that point David quickly conceded, the discussion was over, the ratchet was to trigger, and we were to collectively receive 55% of the deal, and the investors would receive 45%.

It was agreed that Nobuyoshi Yokobori would come to Edinburgh on the 24th and 25th July and then go on to Seattle on the 27th and 28th to progress the deal. I was away on a pre-booked vacation, so Stuart hosted these meetings.

We agreed that Stuart would raise the phasing of payments for our shares. He would stress to Nobuyoshi that it would have a very positive effect on morale and commitment if the initial level of payment to the founders could be 25%, and the subsequent two payments 37.5% of the total amount. We argued that this would not make us rich but would typically allow us to pay off the mortgage on our family homes. Nobuyoshi didn't seem very impressed with this argument, so it seemed to make little progress.

The next stage was that Stuart Harper, Bill Nisen and I were to visit MEI in Osaka in late August 1989.

On Monday morning we were introduced to Mr Yoshikawa, a tall, slim commercial manager. We presented our business plan for a five-year period, showing a need for investment of £1,500,000 investment in the first eight months, and that was quickly approved.

MEI then explained their issues with OWL and OWL International Inc. It had always been their intention to acquire OWL as an R&D centre, but they were concerned by the high-risk nature of our software publishing activities in Seattle in a fast-changing and competitive market. It could easily fail, and this, for MEI, was an unacceptable risk.

Software publishing was not an area in which Matsushita had any experience and they suggested that we should construct the deal so that all our commercial marketing activities should be transferred to Seattle, with up to 49% of OWL International Inc. to be acquired by its staff, and that at a later date it might be spun off.

It seemed clear that what they wanted to buy was our systems development skills rather than our software creation and publishing arm. But bizarrely, they then placed us in their high-tech commercial division, reporting to Mr Yoshikawa.

As part of their due diligence they asked if we had any exclusive deals and we said that it hadn't been our policy to award exclusivity to anybody. The only such deal we had agreed anywhere was a limited-term exclusive deal with MPT for the Japanese market.

Oops!

This was quickly stated to be a big problem, even a deal-buster, and the exclusive agreement with MPT would have to be cancelled before our deal could proceed. Not only that, but I would have to renegotiate our contract with MPT from a position of weakness as we were not allowed to disclose to MPT that we were in the process of selling our company to Matsushita.

One piece of good news, however, was that they had agreed our request that they would purchase an initial 25% of our shares followed by two payments of 37.5%. This was a huge relief for me as I had been under huge pressure from my fellow founders to improve the settlement terms.

Yamaichi UK was represented by Simon Howell – it seems that they had finally realised how incompetent Roderick Seligman was, and I got the impression he had been fired. Also, MEI's senior team had now been joined by a woman, Ms Konishi, who was their in-house corporate lawyer.

The next morning, we assembled for a crucial stage in our talks, but a very noticeable absentee from the MEI team that morning was Nobuyoshi Yokobori. As the main original inspiration behind the deal to buy OWL, this struck us as very odd indeed. We later heard that after our joint dinner the night before he had been so drunk that he had cycled into a lamp-post on his way home, injured himself and broken his glasses.

Our reaction was that this was a very serious, what we would call a 'career-limiting move', as indeed it would have been in the UK or the USA, but to our Japanese hosts this seemed to be just a case of 'these things happen' – his absence, caused by his drunken behaviour, was quite forgivable: 'Boys will be boys'.

We were beginning to learn more about the differing customs and practices in Japan at that time, compared to what was normal in the West. I was struck by the fact that Japanese business was very uncompetitive, at least towards other Japanese companies. For example I suspected the exception in the case of MEI's intransigence regarding MPT's exclusivity rights was simply down to old drinking buddies Yokobori and Yoshimoto being in cahoots to get Yokobori a decent pay-off at our expense.

Jobs were literally held for life; once you joined a company you could pretty much expect it to employ you until you were ready to retire, and companies made no attempt to hire talented managers from other companies. One side-effect of this was that the managers who hadn't been promoted but hadn't been fired were shunted off into a pointless office job called 'madogiwa zoku', which literally means the men who 'sit and look out of the window'.

Japanese companies didn't buy other goods and services from the most competitive supplier but chose to buy from companies in their own 'zaibatsu' – companies that were linked to each other, often by cross-ownership of shares.

It was also clear that women in Japan were often expected to leave work after they got married but if they were unmarried, like Ms Konishi, they were treated exactly the same as the men, an 'honorary man' in effect. I even heard a rumour that Ms Konsihi had been instructed that part of her duties was to take their London lawyers to a Japanese strip club.

On the other hand, there was a refreshing lack of hierarchy. One day on return from lunch we found we couldn't enter the project office as one of the most junior females in the team was in the middle of giving a presentation to her fellow workers. It was her turn to do so.

To be fair, Matsushita had been active in trying to change some of this culture and indeed there was one notable married woman, with children, who retained a position as a respected project manager in the development team.

Another culture that the company was trying to break was the almost universal habit of staying on late every evening drinking with your fellow 'sarariman' –salary men. On our final evening in Osaka we were hosted at dinner by Dr Hiroyuki Mizuno, who was a main Board Director of Matsushita. We were told in advance that Dr Mizuno would leave at 8pm and we shouldn't be offended by this. He was trying to set an example to others in the company that it was a healthier attitude to return to their families in the evening.

Of course, Dr Mizuno's 8pm curfew didn't apply to the rest of us, so we got taken on to the inevitable karaoke bar.

At one point one of our hosts declared "Ritchie-san, you could sing the 'Scottish song'", and they set about riffling through the karaoke records. Eventually the 'Scottish song' was identified and put on the machine. Even though it was in Japanese it didn't take me long to recognise 'Auld Lang Syne'; I could even remember most of the words.

Once we'd settled in and had a few drinks the Matsushita executives began to open up a little. A few of them had grown-up daughters who were now living in the West – in France, the UK and the USA – because they found the restrictions on career opportunities for females in Japan too restrictive. Even the Japanese were pushing against these cultural norms.

WE SET about trying to resolve the MPT exclusivity issue. Somewhat irritatingly, Masuo Yoshimoto confirmed that they had comfortably exceeded the revenue target for the first year of our arrangement and so under the terms of our contract they were entitled to retain their exclusivity. Ironically, this had been largely achieved by their obtaining a fat contract with Matsushita, but they had also progressed good relationships with Sanyo and Fujitsu.

As this was a commercial distribution deal, it was really the responsibility of OWL International Inc. (the Edinburgh-based salespeople reported to the Bellevue office, keeping the division between the roles of the two offices clear), so Bill Nisen arranged to travel to Tokyo in late September to try to agree the changes in the relationship between OWL International Inc. and MPT. Our proposal was to tell Yoshimoto that the parent company, Office Workstations Limited, was in discussions to be sold; unfortunately, we couldn't officially tell him who the purchaser was, even though it seemed obvious from his close relationship with his student buddy Nobuyoshi Yokobori that he almost certainly did know. Bill told Yoshimoto that as a result of this acquisition, OWL International Inc. would lose the exclusive rights to the Guide products. Therefore OWL International Inc. was no longer going to be able to extend future exclusivity arrangements to MPT.

Bill spent several days trying to make progress with Yoshimoto but the Japanese are famous for being uncomfortable with making quick decisions and he prevaricated. I was called in to join Bill on October 2nd to try and move this along. We had regular catch-up meetings with Masuo but we inevitably found ourselves spending most of the time hanging around Tokyo. MPT's offices in Tokyo consisted of two modest rooms where over 20 engineers shared about 10 desks, and the Japanese custom of taking your outdoor shoes off at the entrance to an indoor space lent the offices a bit of an interesting aroma.

Bill and I decided one night that we would go out and 'get into trouble' in Tokyo. Fortunately, we had no real idea of how to do that, but Bill remembered the location of a bar to which he had been taken by Toshiba. We went there and stayed for about an hour, during which time we bought some drinks, including for our hosts. After a while we realised this wasn't much fun so we decided to leave, at which point we were a bit surprised to be presented with a bill for $300.

Later we told our colleagues at Matsushita about this rip-off behaviour, but they assured us that we hadn't been ripped off at all, and a $300 bill was perfectly normal at one of these bars.

Bill went back to Seattle and I ended up spending a total of 10 days in Tokyo, visiting Masuo most days trying to move to a conclusion on our proposed deal, but mostly I was forced to hang around Tokyo, filling in time. All this international travel was taking its toll on me, and I had picked up some form of bronchitis, presumably on one of my long flights.

After over a week of this, we eventually agreed with them that MPT would retain exclusivity of the current product, Guide 2.0, but would not have exclusive rights over future products, although we agreed to appoint them as non-exclusive distributors for our products for the next five years. As compensation for giving up future exclusivity we would make them a payment of $350,000 – Masuo drove a hard bargain.

There was then a discussion with MEI but they were unhappy about any deal including rights to sell Guidex so I had to return to Tokyo on October 30th to try and renegotiate the deal. At least by this time MEI had agreed to be identified as the acquiring party and Masuo was clearly very interested in maintaining a good relationship with them. I finally managed to agree terms acceptable to both MPT and MEI on November 2nd.

On 9th November 1989, David Thomson, Stuart Harper, Bill Nisen and I were back in the London offices of Lovell White Durrant to tie up any loose ends and finalise the deal. My coughing fits were getting worse; if I started one it was very difficult to stop, which was rather alarming to anybody who was with me at the time.

We were somewhat surprised that there were two individuals new to us at this meeting. Mr Nakajima, a very senior member of the main board of Matsushita, and a heavyweight New York lawyer from Weil, Gotshal and Manges; apparently

they were Matsushita's US legal counsel. Under the circumstances, we expected the meeting to start with opening remarks
by Mr Nakajima as the most senior Matsushita executive;
however, the New York lawyer, who looked as though he had
had more than the one facelift over the years – he seemed to
find it very difficult to move very much of his face – opened the
meeting by saying he was new to the deal but that MEI had
invited him in to advise them.

His advice to them was that there was no way that we were
worth £8 million; that we were still at a very early stage and our
business model was mostly unproven, had demonstrated relatively poor revenues so far, and that our risk of failure was still
quite high. He therefore suggested that a price of £6 million
was much more appropriate than the £8 million that had been
agreed.

We expressed considerable surprise at this turn of events.
We said that we had never sought any interest from, or asked to
be bought by, MEI; that they had approached us. We had
always said that our price was £8 million if they wanted to do a
deal, but if they didn't, we were quite happy to continue as an
independent company.

We said we were very sorry that we and MEI had
completely wasted our time over the last year, and we all stood
up, as one, to leave the room.

Mr Yoshikawa seemed alarmed by this and spoke quickly.
He said that Mr Nakajima, their main Board Director, had travelled especially from Osaka to attend this meeting and he
thought we should extend him the courtesy of proceeding with
the meeting.

The proposed £2 million price drop was never discussed
again, the price went back, silently, to £8 million, and the New
York lawyer played no further part in the meeting.

There were one or two things to resolve but the biggest

issue was the deal done with MPT, particularly the compensation payment agreed of $350,000. MEI thought that we should entirely bear this cost and proposed to adjust the acquisition price by that amount. I protested that the agreement with MPT had significant advantages to MEI as well as ourselves and that we should split the cost between us. In the end £150,000 was taken off the sale price.

So, the final price for MEI to buy OWL was agreed at £7.85 million.

We had to be sure that the deal was constructed to make sure that we founders weren't liable for capital gains tax, then at a rate of 40% of the full sale price, even though 75% of the price was to be delayed by up to five years. This was especially important to me as my wife Barbara was now a very senior tax inspector; indeed, at that time she was in charge of Centre 1, the largest tax office in Europe, which was responsible for the personal tax affairs of all 2.2 million Scottish taxpayers. This included me and all my fellow OWLers. We had to ensure that our tax affairs were all completely and unambiguously legal.

At the time of selling, Office Workstations Limited had 71 employees and OWL international Inc. had another 18, so another issue to be sorted was that of staff stock options. We had had a stock option plan for all staff, but during the last 16 months while we had been in negotiations with MEI it had not been legally possible for us to issue fresh options to staff who had joined the company over that time. Stuart Harper came up with the suggestion that we founders should, between us, chip into a fund of £125,000 to be distributed among them as a form of 'shadow options'.

I was delighted that every one of the founders immediately agreed to do this on a pro rata basis, so that all our staff would benefit to some extent from the sale of the business. Unfortunately, there was no way of avoiding the fact that we founders had to pay tax on all the value received, including the money we passed on as compensation for these shadow options.

After the London meetings were successfully concluded, Mr Nakajima, Yoshikawa and Yokobori decided to visit our Edinburgh offices the very next day, Friday, 10th November. We gave them a tour of our offices and took them to dinner at the Vintner Rooms, a restaurant on the ground floor of the oldest commercial building in Leith – premises that had originally been used to import fine claret wine from the Bordeaux area of France during the eighteenth century. This building was shared with the Scotch Malt Whisky Society upstairs, where the very finest individual whisky casks are selected and bottled in exclusive batches for their members. The Japanese were very impressed by the fine whiskies on offer. It was an excellent choice.

Before dinner we had been quietly told that Mr Nakajima liked to drink very fine wine and that Matsushita would be picking up the bill for the meal, so we gave Bill Nisen the task of choosing an excellent bottle of wine – at an appropriately high price. When the bottle arrived with a certain amount of ceremony, it was opened, and a small amount was poured for tasting. Unfortunately, it had turned into vinegar. A second bottle of the same wine was brought from the cellar only for us to discover that it was also undrinkable. We felt a bit sorry for the restaurant, who had just been forced to write off what had probably been the two most expensive bottles in their cellar.

The formal completion meeting at MEI's headquarters in Osaka was scheduled for Monday, 18th December, and our team was to be David Thomson and myself, accompanied by John Rafferty, the managing partner of our lawyers, WJ Burness. All three of us flew out to Osaka. This visit was largely a ceremonial one and included a very special dinner at a restaurant in the shadow of Osaka Castle.

The completion meeting was just a signing session, all the negotiations having been completed. David brought along powers of attorney from the other investors, and he signed on his own and their behalf. However, my powers of attorney were for all the other shareholders in OWL, every single one of them, including all our staff who were option holders. Signing the documents so many times completely ruined my signature, which to this day has been reduced to a squiggly line.

Ms Konishi, observing David Thomson and me signing the acquisition documents

That evening I was amused to observe the two uptight British lawyers, John Hiscock of Lovell White Durrant and John Rafferty of WJ Burness, performing at the inevitable late evening karaoke session.

Sealing the deal with Mr Nakajima

The deal was consummated. We were now a subsidiary of Matsushita, the largest consumer electronics company in the world.

19

TURNING JAPANESE

After the acquisition was completed, we started on building a deeper relationship with our new owners in Osaka. Martin Smith and Phil Cooke were the first engineers from OWL since our acquisition by MEI to make the trip to Japan. In early 1990 they spent about 10 days in Osaka and Tokyo, giving courses on Guide and touring various R&D labs.

After the 15 months of negotiation before the deal was completed, we were surprised that Matsushita seemed now to be confused about quite what to do with us. Although the original idea for the acquisition had come from Nobuyoshi Yokobori in the R&D function at MEI, we didn't immediately develop a close technical development relationship with them, and we were quickly placed into the category of a subsidiary commercial businesses, sharing our main Board Director, Mr Yoshikawa, with their other, completely unrelated, hardware subsidiary, Solbourne, a Californian workstation company.

Yoshi Hiriyama was assigned to work with us in Edinburgh and Bellevue, which we welcomed warmly; Yoshi was a great guy. We were encouraged to continue to develop our commercial activity, but we didn't have any opportunity to have any strategic discussions about how Matsushita could make best use of our technology within their wider corporate ambitions.

The year after they bought us, Matsushita made the much larger acquisition of Universal Studios in Hollywood, one of the largest of the US film production companies. This whole initiative seemed to have been driven by the fact that Sony had already bought Columbia, another major Hollywood studio, and Matsushita was clearly worried about maintaining their position against their traditional rivals and gaining control over what they judged to be valuable content which could be played on their various entertainment platforms. From the outside, this might have looked like MEI were trying to become more competitive, but in fact it was more of a copycat move. They just didn't want to lose out to Sony.

We, however, were excited and intrigued by the acquisition, and we suggested to MEI that we could potentially develop some attractive multimedia content with Universal Studios. We were quickly told that on no account should we contact anybody at Universal and that all decisions about what we should do were to come from Osaka.

Unlike Sony, which had (and still has) a more delegated management structure, Matsushita was strictly a top-down organisation. All roads led, in this case, to Osaka, and all developments, especially anything which contained innovation, was to be directed by them. This was quite a contrast to how we had originally set up and run our business.

It was a shame, as we could have developed some very appealing products.

In the end, Universal Studios didn't work out for MEI and it was sold on after five years.

IN EARLY 1990, I got a call from the Bank of Scotland: could we pop up for a meeting?

Over the years the Bank of Scotland had always been happy to lunch us in style at their magnificent headquarters on the Mound, often hosted by Gavin Masterton, now the Managing Director of the bank. They had always been willing to allow us a sizable overdraft as long as it was more than twice covered by our receivables – the money that our customers owed us at any given time. Before we sold our business to Matsushita our Non-Executive Directors had usually been amazed at the level of debt that the Bank of Scotland was comfortable with us carrying. In effect, the bank was often effectively the largest stakeholder in our business, but without any equity ownership. I had always suspected that the unseen hand of Gavin was behind the scenes, silently supporting us.

But at this meeting the mood had unexpectedly changed. We were told that the corporate policy of the Bank of Scotland had been revised and from that point on they could only count UK-based debtors as collateral to cover our overdraft.

"That's a shame," I remarked, "because about 85% of our business is international." The various organisations that owed us money weren't small outfits, but well-known multinationals like Ford, Data General, Bell Atlantic and so on; surely they were sound enough to provide strong cover for our overdraft?

Apparently not.

It seemed to me completely incredible that the Bank of Scotland, who had supported us through thick and thin, including at times when our US subsidiary wasn't going well, when there was a realistic chance that we could go bust, should withdraw support now that we were a subsidiary of Matsushita, the largest consumer electronics company in the world with a market capitalisation of over $60 billion and cash reserves of $7 billion. Even if Matsushita did ever decide to close us down, they would undoubtedly clear all their debts first; as they had indicated before, major Japanese corporations like Matsushita were very honourable in this way.

For the first time in five years, the bank was no longer at any risk whatsoever of losing any money because of their exposure in OWL, and yet they decided to pull our overdraft.

Since the takeover, we had been approached by a few Japanese banks who were keen for our business, so I was able to take a relaxed attitude to the Bank of Scotland shooting itself in the foot in this way. Within a few weeks we had transferred our overdraft facility to Sumitomo Bank at an interest rate well below what any UK bank would have given us.

IT WAS ARRANGED that we would have our first post-acquisition board meeting in Bellevue and a whole bunch of us went over to attend it. For various reasons we didn't all travel on the same airline but due to bad weather the main Seattle–Tacoma airport was closed, and planes were being diverted elsewhere. A few of us were diverted to Portland, Oregon, others to Vancouver, and bussed back to Seattle. Bill Nisen ended up landing at Boeing Field, the landing strip attached to the Boeing 737 factory in Everett on the south side of Seattle. On the face of it that should have been the best outcome, but unfortunately it took Boeing over three hours to find a set of steps that could allow the passengers to leave that aircraft.

The board meeting mainly consisted of us outlining our proposed plans for the future development of our hypertext business. Since it looked as though – despite MEI having said they wanted the sales and marketing side of OWL separated and potentially later spun off – they had placed us in a commercial division of Matsushita, the board were mostly interested in hearing about that. They didn't really question our plans as they really didn't have any experience of these markets.

After the board meeting and dinner, we assembled in a tequila bar where we were all required to have shots of tequila. When my turn came there was only a little tequila left in the bottle, but the worm was still there, so unfortunately it was down to me to drink the tequila complete with the worm. When faced with such situations, the Japanese way is to get on with it and conform. At least the worm was very well pickled.

WE HAD RECEIVED our fresh investment from MEI and we were encouraged to launch a marketing campaign to encourage users to try Guide, so as to build up our business.

Our Product Manager in Bellevue, Alister Gibson, was charged with developing this campaign. Alister had transferred to our US office to undertake the product marketing role there and his wife Debra had become a very effective personal assistant to the senior management team in Bellevue.

It hadn't been easy persuading Alister and Debra to relocate to Bellevue for Debra, although she was Scottish, she had been brought up for several years in the Midwest of the USA, where her father's employment was based, and, remembering the brutal winters she had experienced there, she was very reluctant to go back. Eventually we persuaded her that the winters in Seattle were much milder, very similar to those in Scotland, in fact, and she eventually agreed to move.

Alister did some research and market testing and concluded that we were still in evangelist mode, and that very little of our profitable revenue came from selling Guide, our core hypertext product. Instead, our most valuable business came from undertaking major OEM projects for companies such as Hewlett-Packard and Bell Atlantic, or specific specially engineered projects such as at the Dallas Theological Seminary.

He reasoned that if we could reach out to more people in the first place, we should be better placed to gain more business opportunities. He designed a marketing campaign where the first 5,000 applicants who contacted us could get a free limited version of our software and a professionally produced demonstration video. This was to be backed up by an extensive advertising campaign in the trade press.

We assembled one morning in our Bellevue office to build these demonstration packs. Each one was to contain some documentation, a software disk and a demonstration video.

In retrospect this free demonstration pack turned out to be a terrible idea. It emerged that most of the purchasers of our $495 Guide product were using it to experiment with the concept of hypertext, and several of them would get in touch with us if they needed us to develop something more elaborate. But when we supplied them with a free demo disk, they were happy to settle for that and not bother to buy our product.

The sales of our packaged product dropped dramatically. I later wondered if we should prepare a case study for a business school – a £1 million marketing campaign that led to fewer sales.

Because we weren't a major product category, we always had a struggle to maintain our distribution channels. In those days, most software retail in the USA was dominated by Egghead stores – a dedicated chain of software retail outlets that had branches all over the metropolitan USA. Fortunately for us, the headquarters of Egghead was based in the nearby town of Issaquah and we made a point of befriending the various executives there and buying them a few beers from time to time, persuading them that our very different software product added valuable variety to their offerings. Frankly, that strategy kept us on the shelves in Egghead much longer than the level of our sales deserved.

MICROSOFT WERE LAUNCHING A NEW, improved version of Windows – Windows 3.0 – regarded by many in the industry as the first version of Windows that was sufficiently robust for real business use. They had asked us to develop a hypertext demonstration disk which could be distributed to explain the benefits and features of this new system and we were very happy to have the endorsement of Microsoft in choosing us for this demo disk.

Guide 3.1 for Microsoft Windows 3

The launch of Windows 3.0 was to be held at the Center City Theater at Columbus Circle in New York on 22nd May 1990, and we were invited to attend and demonstrate Guide. A number of other software development companies were also showing products designed to run on this new system. Bill Gates did his launch presentation, backed up by a slick video sequence, and we were to show the next version of our Guide product, Guide 3.1, in our demonstration station in the side corridors of the theatre along with all the other vendors.

Paul Allen, the original co-founder of Microsoft with Bill Gates, who had suffered a cancer scare in the early 1980s and left the company at that time, had started a new software company, Asymmetrix. We were aware that Asymmetrix had developed a product, ToolBook, which could be used to develop e-learning projects on a fixed card format similar to Apple's Hypercard.

This competed to some extent with parts of our market for the development of e-learning projects, such as the one we developed at Cornell University medical school.

What we hadn't anticipated was that a demonstration copy of ToolBook would be bundled with every Windows 3.0 system shipped. There was obviously still a significant benefit of Paul Allen having been the co-founder, a major shareholder, and still on the board of Microsoft. We couldn't compete with such an inside job.

We also became aware that Microsoft sales staff had been telling customers that for hypertext document delivery for applications such as technical support they probably didn't need to use Guide, but might be perfectly happy with a simple Windows Help utility supplied by Microsoft which was designed to develop interactive online support information.

Once again it appeared that major software giants were determined to try to put us out of business? Actually, although it often felt that way, it wasn't really. They were focused on building their business, and if you got squashed along the way it was just an accident.

Pierre Trudeau, the Canadian Prime Minister once said, speaking of the USA, that Canada's relationship with the United States was like that of 'a mouse in bed with an elephant'. If, for any reason best known to them they wanted to roll over, it was the little guy that got hurt. Usually, they had no idea of the damage they were causing.

Another new product launch that was somewhat competitive with us was Lotus Notes, an interactive information publishing platform from the formidable Lotus company, most famous for their spreadsheet package Lotus 1-2-3. It was initially launched at a price of $495, the same price as Guide. We always struggled with how to price our product so we were intrigued with this pricing decision and got in touch with a contact at Lotus who confirmed that the reason they had set that price was that it was the price at we were selling Guide. Even if we hadn't thought of them as a direct competitor, I guess they were thinking differently.

We did have some more promising breakthroughs. We had been contacted by Jerry Goguen of Data General to develop a substantial product which they wanted to call Intellibook. Intellibook was based on our Guidex architecture but used Unix servers to deliver hypermedia materials to PCs. Also a German distributor called Computer 2000 agreed to translate and publish a German version of Guide.

IN AUGUST 1990 we hosted our board meeting in Edinburgh during the Edinburgh International Festival, the largest arts and cultural festival in the world. Knowing that the Japanese were keen to enjoy world-class experiences, we booked to attend a ballet featuring Rudolf Nureyev, by far the best-known male ballet dancer of the twentieth century. We thought it was a particularly good idea to book a no-dialogue ballet so our Japanese guests could just relax and enjoy the dancing.

Unfortunately, it soon became quite clear that the Japanese had absolutely no knowledge of who Nureyev was, his fame having completely passed them by, and the experience wasn't helped by the fact that Nureyev was at the very end of his career and seemed to have lost most of his athletic ability and dancing prowess.

The next night we took them to a Fringe show, a big alternative circus called Archaos, again thinking of minimising the language barrier. One of the acts involved a clown throwing wet fish towards a member of the audience selected at random, who was required to catch the fish in a bucket. We weren't sitting anywhere near the front, but unfortunately the clown came right up into the audience and selected me to be the fish catcher.

One of the cultural expectations with the Japanese is that when it is your turn to perform (such as in a karaoke session or drinking the worm in a tequila) you are expected to do your best to perform.

So I did my best to perform, and hammed up the task of catching wet fish in a bucket. I seemed to make a bigger impression on our Japanese guests than Rudolf Nureyev had.

Matsushita held its annual kick-off meeting in Osaka in early January and I was invited to join the 1991 one. I flew to Osaka and joined thousands of other Matsushita employees in a huge sports hall near the R&D HQ buildings. As an 'important' manager of an international subsidiary I was seated at the very front of the room among the other gaijins (the non-Japanese). We were all amused that this massive session was opened by all of us, including us foreigners, being required to leap to our feet three times, throw our hands above our heads and shout 'banzai'.

~

WE HAD FURTHER DEVELOPED our suite of professional publishing solutions, eventually releasing our comprehensive set of document management tools under the name Guide

Professional Publisher, which we sold for a list price of $20,000, and we continued to attract heavyweight online publishing projects.

It was a little ironic that we ended up as a business in a market very close to where we had targeted at the start. Our original concept had been to build a system that would allow professional teams of technical authors to build large collections of documents. Along the way we had diverted to these documents being dynamic, or hypertext, rather than predominantly on paper, but we ended up providing a solution for the market we had originally identified, the professional large-volume technical publishing market.

We developed a factory documentation system for Compugraphics which allowed them to track electronic documents instead of paper-based ones, throughout a clean-room environment, and we also went on to develop an electronic manual system for a company called Lam Research Corporation whose equipment – plasma-etching machines – are also typically deployed in clean-room situations.

We developed for the scientific publisher Elsevier an interactive 'Active Library on Corrosion' which enabled technical staff to identify corrosion on-site by reading our multimedia guide. For consumer manufacturer Procter & Gamble we created an information support system for operators of their various manufacturing processes.

In the field of education, we won a small but prestigious contract from the UK educational supplier Research Machines, to provide a hypertext guide on CD-ROM to a new exhibition at the British Museum on the subject of 'The Making of England'. This project gave us several jumping-off points in terms of the combination of linear and hierarchic structuring of information, and how users navigate through them.

These projects became vital inputs to later designing a DVD authoring platform for Matsushita as part of the DVD consortium, but as we developed these and other solutions we were aware that, although we were now growing our revenue dramatically, it would be a very long time before we could possibly build any kind of business that could be regarded as significant to a massive consumer electronics business like Panasonic.

MEI had also finally realised what had seemed to us to be obvious from the start – that although our software development skills could be immensely valuable to major Matsushita projects, our commercial operations wouldn't even move their dial, especially as the hypertext market at that time was still firmly stuck in early adopter mode.

It was eventually determined, as they had stated during the acquisition process, that we should spin off our commercial business and redirect our software development activities exclusively towards MEI's R&D needs.

Bill Nisen was charged with finding suitable acquirers in the USA with the help of corporate advisory company Broadview Associates, and I started simultaneous discussions in Edinburgh with Derek Gray, now a senior Vice-President at Adobe. Bill spoke with Dataware, Claris, Fulcrum Technologies, Bell Atlantic and Frame Technologies, and I was making good progress with Derek Gray, who had always had an interest in our hypertext activities and could clearly envisage where we would fit within the Adobe operation.

In the end, MEI asked us to close down all these discussions; they had decided to sell the business to its current management team as they had previously indicated they might do. Maybe they were worried that if acquired by another corporation, OWL International Inc. would go on to some success and cause them some embarrassment. For me it was a shame as I'm sure OWL could have prospered under Adobe, who were at that time developing their Acrobat architecture for paperless documents which has since – via its PDF format – become the industry standard.

For me, it seemed obvious by mid-1992 that I was no longer needed in OWL. I had led the commercial development of the company and Stuart Harper had led the engineering activities. As it was the engineering function that was to continue under MEI and the Bellevue-based commercial business was to be hived off, I had effectively become redundant. Richard Stonehouse and I both negotiated our exit from the business, and we left the company on 31st October 1992.

Bill Nisen decided not to buy in to OWL International Inc. and Jim Culbertson and Rick Dillhoff took over the management of the business, which they renamed InfoAccess Inc. They were no longer connected to OWL, but were allowed to continue selling OWL technology. The InfoAccess launch was finally announced on 12th April 1993.

Initially InfoAccess sold the Guide range of technology, including landing a large automobile technical manual publishing system with General Motors, making it a supplier to both Ford and GM, the two giants of the US automobile industry.

Over the next few years InfoAccess also developed and sold a Web publishing tool called HTML Transit to exploit the fast-growing Web tools market. InfoAccess was ultimately sold to Intranet Solutions in September 1999 in a deal worth $14 million.

UNDER THE DIRECTION of MEI's R&D division, OWL continued to provide key technology, including the development of the software architecture behind the DVD video publishing format.

In an attempt to avoid a repeat of the costly and destructive VHS/Betamax battle, a single DVD standard was agreed between the main players in the audio/video market: Sony, Panasonic and Philips. MEI proposed their OWL subsidiary as the developer of the architecture for the DVD platform. Because of this, every time anyone anywhere in the world puts a DVD into a DVD player and choses from an on-screen menu (to select sections, scenes, trailers and so on), they are using the software developed in Edinburgh by Panasonic OWL for the DVD consortium.

Although I had left by this point, I was still, naturally, interested in what Panasonic OWL were doing. They also developed several interfaces for various cable TV set-top boxes for MEI, but were never really asked to exploit OWL's leading-edge hypertext or multimedia publishing skills, even when it was becoming obvious that the World Wide Web was beginning to take over the world.

For my own part, I was very disappointed that Panasonic did not have the imagination or nerve to create a genuinely innovative product. Over the years I had concluded that for hypertext publishing to really succeed as a replacement for paper-based publishing it would have to become ubiquitous.

This was the thinking behind Apple's making Hypercard effectively free, and Adobe's decision to make PDF an open standard, and our own decision to allow people to publish documents royalty-free in read-only Guide Envelope format and, of course, some five years later the World Wide Web became a popular open standard that was free to be used by all without any restrictions.

When we agreed to sell our business to Matsushita I had envisaged that we might collectively work to design a portable electronic book device, Panasonic being mostly an electronic equipment manufacturer. Potentially this could have been an early version of a device that might have become like a Kindle e-book product.

I had observed the recent arrival on the market of the Nintendo Game Boy, a battery-powered low-cost hand-held games device with a built-in display. I had also noticed the huge popularity of Manga comics among the Japanese population – piles of them were stacked up at the railway station newsstands – and I had envisaged that we might easily develop a powerful portable hand-held Manga comic publishing device, after which later versions could be enhanced to finally become an effective book publishing device for the global market. We could have built the Kindle before the Kindle.

Of course I was wrong in expecting Panasonic to even consider such innovative products – innovation was really not in their DNA. Sony was the innovative company of the two – after all, it created the Walkman portable music player and thus single-handedly created a whole new product sector.

20

THE CUCKOO LURKING IN THE HYPERTEXT NEST

I n late November 1990 OWL took part in the first European Conference on Hypertext, known as ECHT. It was a technical conference with a small exhibition attached held in Versailles on the outskirts of Paris.

Professor Peter Brown made the opening keynote presentation at the conference, and we demonstrated our Guide and Guidex hypertext technology at the exhibition, where we were supported by Frame, our French distributors.

It was at this that when Tim Berners-Lee sought me out. Tim was a second-generation computer professional, the son of two mathematicians who had met while working in the early days of the computer industry in the 1950s. Tim went on to earn a Physics degree at Oxford in 1976, and in early 1980s, as a consultant at CERN, he had been experimenting with a program he had written, called Enquire, inspired by a concept which he explained thus:

> *Suppose all the information stored on computers everywhere were linked. Suppose I could program my computer to create a space in which anything could be linked to anything. All the bits of informa-*

tion in every computer at CERN, and on the planet, would be avail-
able to me and anyone else. There would be a single, global
information space.

In 1984 he gained a fellowship at CERN and was able, to
some extent, to progress this vision. In March 1989 he laid out
his proposition for what would become the Web in a document
called 'Information Management: A Proposal'. His boss at the
time, Mike Sendall, wrote the words, 'Vague but exciting' on
the cover of the proposal. The Web never became an official
CERN project, but Mike allocated Tim some time to work on it.

Crucially, one key section of Tim's 'Proposal' states:

> *discussions on hypertext have sometimes tackled the problem of*
> *copyright enforcement and data security. These are of secondary*
> *importance at CERN, where information exchange is still more*
> *important than secrecy. Authorisation and accounting systems for*
> *hypertext could conceivably be designed which are very sophisti-*
> *cated, but they are not proposed here. In cases where reference*
> *must be made to data which is in fact protected, existing file protec-*
> *tion systems should be sufficient.*

Arguably the digital world is still coping with the implications of this decision. The Web was created with no attempt to
include protection for copyright ownership or personal identity
and secrecy. Unlike Ted Nelson's Xanadu design, it was to be
open and free – a laudable dream, but one which inherently
carried with it a dark side.

On the other hand, the very simplicity of the Web – a
linking mechanism between any two places in any two documents – was undoubtedly a clear factor in its success. What I
didn't realise when Tim approached me, as it only emerged
over the next few years, was that Berners-Lee's World Wide
Web was to behave a bit like a young cuckoo, pushing all its

rivals out of the nest, eventually becoming the dominant hyper-text solution delivered on the internet.

By late November 1990 he had a simple version of his Web working on his NeXT computer in his office which demon-strated navigation between documents; however, his system only had a relatively primitive way of displaying the docu-ments. He had determined that all CERN needed at that time was a tool capable of distributing text documents formatted for a screen with 24 rows of 80 characters apiece, and indeed his documents were displayed in plain text only, with no layout, typefaces, embedded photos or graphics.

His hypertext links were fired by pressing a numbered key on the keyboard corresponding to a number shown in bold inserted in the document. However, Tim had previously observed Hypercard and he knew that a more sophisticated interface was clearly desirable.

He had come to the Versailles hypertext conference to seek potential collaborators to help with improving the user experi-ence of his system, and he had sought me out. He describes this meeting in his book *Weaving the Web*, published in 1999:

> *Undaunted, in September 1990 Robert and I went to the European Conference on Hypertext Technology (ECHT) at Versailles to pitch the idea. The conference exhibition was small, but there were a number of products on display, such as a multimedia training manual for repairing a car.*
>
> *I approached Ian Ritchie and the folks from Owl Ltd. which had a product called Guide. In Peter Brown's original Guide work at the University of Southampton, when a user clicked on a hyper-text link, the new document would be inserted right there in place. The version now commercialized by Owl looked astonishingly like what I had envisioned for a Web browser, the program that would open and display documents, and preferably let people edit them, too. All that was missing was the Internet.*

They've already done the difficult bit! I thought, so I tried to persuade them to add an Internet connection. They were friendly enough, but they, too, were unconvinced.

He made a couple of trivial mistakes here – the conference was held in late November, not September as stated, and Peter Brown was based at the University of Kent at Canterbury, not Southampton.

Unfortunately, it really wasn't possible for us to collaborate with Tim on such an informal and unfunded project. Back in 1990, the internet, which underpinned Tim's Web technology, wasn't available to us, or to anybody else outside the public sector world of government, defence and academic research.

There was consequently no commercial market for internet-based software, so a company like us had no effective way of selling products to this community. Also, now that we were a subsidiary of Matsushita, there was no possibility of our being allowed to develop such a solution for some form of 'public good' without a strong prospect of a future commercial return, and at that time, there was no expectation of the internet being opened to the rest of us.

I was, however, intrigued by Tim's level of ambition, which was extraordinary. Even at this time, when his system existed only on the single computer in his office, he seemed completely convinced that his World Wide Web would take over the world one day and be adopted widely by everybody for everyday information sharing. For an internal project at a research centre for particle physics this seemed a rather over inflated estimate of the potential for his system.

He had heard that we had developed a markup language, HML, and he subsequently requested information about it in the following fax . . .

From Tim Berners-Lee

CN Division, CERN, 1211 Geneva 23,
Switzerland

31 May 91

To: Ian Ritchie

Office Workstations Limited

144 Broughton Rd

Edinburgh EH7 4LE

Fax +44(31)557 5721

Ian,

At last I get to send this, some time after our
phone call. Please send us, for 'Guidance'
(assuming this to be a superset of Guide)

Price and ordering information for a single
evaluation copy, and any indication of larger
volume arrangements;

As full documentation as possible;

Details of your HML format, so that we can
consider compatibility with our own SGML
browsers;

Details of scripts which can be attached to
links, so that we can investigate the possibility
of interfacing to our own information access
tools.

We have someone who is currently evaluating
hypertext products, and so we expect to order
an evaluation copy immediately.

Thanks in advance

Tim BL

Naturally, I was happy to send him the information he
requested, including the HML specification.

Of course, he could have asked CERN to commission us to develop a front-end browser for their Web, a task we could very easily have done at quite a modest cost. After all, we had built specialised hypertext browser solutions for Hewlett-Packard, Data General and Bell Atlantic. But Tim's Web was not an 'official' project at CERN and there didn't seem to be a budget allocated for such a project.

CERN's policy regarding software systems was generally 'buy, not build'. However, this policy alone is not the only reason CERN did not enthusiastically take up Tim Berners-Lee's World Wide Web project. According to David Williams, the leader of the Computing and Networks Division at CERN, Berners-Lee focused a lot of his persuasive efforts on the hypertext aspects of the Web, but there were several people at CERN, Williams included, who did not feel that hypertext was a particularly appropriate way to represent and navigate scientific information.

In any case, with our product Guidex, we had already developed a large-scale, sophisticated hypertext system that operated very effectively over computer networks – commercial private ones at the time – and could very easily have been ported to the internet.

Our markup language, HML, was designed to represent the inherent structure of documents, and not just the simple hypertext links as in HTML – as a result the early Web didn't build in metadata information, which was later corrected with the development of the more comprehensive XML standard.

By Christmas 1990, Tim had the World Wide Web software up and running at CERN in its most basic form, and by 6th August 1991, people outside CERN, such as their particle accelerator colleagues at Stanford University, got access to the Web as a public internet service for the first time.

After the 1990 European hypertext conference at Versailles, the decision was made to hold future conferences under the auspices of the ACM, the US-based international association for computing researchers. Conferences on even years were to be held in Europe and odd years in the USA.

The ACM Hypertext 91 conference was held in Austin, Texas and I was asked to be a member of the programme committee. I was somewhat dismayed when a paper submitted by Tim Berners-Lee and Robert Cailliau, his collaborator on the Web project, was turned down by the committee.

As an industry participant I was always keen to have practical projects represented at the conference, but I was outvoted by the academics, who determined that Tim's system addressed few of the issues facing the hypertext systems of the time, particularly link consistency. When contents move in a system, links that point to the contents can become broken. Many hypertext systems were designed to deal with this problem; the Web, on the other hand, had completely ignored this issue.

So, Tim's paper was judged insufficiently innovative to be included in the conference programme, but Tim and Robert attended the conference anyway and tried to interest the hypertext community in their project without, as he later reported, much success.

THE FOLLOWING year the ACM hypertext conference was back in Europe and the ECHT92 event was held in Milan, Italy. I had been asked to deliver the opening keynote speech, which I saw as a huge honour and took very seriously, spending hours on the preparation and development of my slides, all 84 of them, many of them including graphics.

I wanted to use computer slides rather than a carousel of old-fashioned 35mm slides but there was no easy way of transporting such a large slide set; in those days such a large file could not be emailed, would have required a huge number of floppy disks, and I couldn't depend on the conference organisers to provide a CD-ROM device. I therefore decided to take a bulky external hard drive which could be plugged into an Apple Mac. Today, it could be emailed in seconds, or taken on a USB flash drive.

I flew to Milan on Sunday and checked in at the conference venue. My hard disk drive was plugged in and working just fine so I was all set for the next morning, Monday, 30th November, when I would be opening the conference with my keynote.

I had decided to challenge the delegates to consider why hypertext hadn't yet taken off as a widely adopted technology, and I decided to use an analogy – comparing aspects of the Industrial Revolution (1750–1850) with the current Information Revolution (1945–).

I described the first phase of the Industrial Revolution with the development of the canal network. Canals revolutionised the transportation of goods, along the way developing a whole set of new technologies, including the construction of cuttings, tunnels and bridges. I pointed out that our equivalent new technologies, such as high-quality displays, processing power and speedy communications links, were still relatively primitive and awkward to use, a bit like during the canal age.

I then described the next phase of the Industrial Revolution, which was exemplified by the arrival of the railways. The railway industry used all the technologies that had been developed for the canal system – the cuttings, tunnels and bridges – but it was so much more efficient that it very quickly completely replaced canals as the primary means of transportation.

The canal engineers had developed the basic technology, but it was the railways that exploited them and became the primary means of communication, wiping out the commercial canal market along the way.

I told the Milan audience "we are currently in the canal age of the information publishing revolution", that the railway age would arrive sometime soon from somewhere and that our engineering achievements would be of value when hypertext finally took off and became universal, as I believed it inevitably would.

I then went on to summarise the technology adoption model explained in Geoffrey Moore's book *Crossing the Chasm*, which had been published the year before, in 1991. Geoffrey Moore had described how the 'early adopter' market and the 'majority' markets often didn't connect up, and that there was usually a chasm between them. More often than not, technology has a burst of interest in the early adopter market, but then its effectiveness has to be proven before it can be adopted by the wider community – the majority market.

I explained that it seemed to me that the hypertext community was currently in the chasm – the early adopter market had happened, but the real market was still to take off.

Back in 1992, I genuinely had no inkling that the modern railway equivalent of my analogy would come from Tim's World Wide Web, which was still mostly invisible, even to the hypertext community. -

But that was all soon to change.

During 1992, the US Congress passed the 'Scientific and Advanced-Technology Act', which opened up internet access to computer networks which were not used exclusively for research and education purposes. Various commercial businesses started providing key internet-carried services to the public such as email. Over the next few months, the various established dial-up commercial network systems, such as CompuServe and America Online in the USA, and Minitel in France, came under pressure to allow their users access to the internet to address the widest possible community, initially by developing email links between them. Microsoft had even been in the process of developing their own private commercial network called Microsoft Network (MSN), but they abandoned it when it became clear that such private proprietary networks were no longer going to succeed. (The final restrictions on carrying commercial traffic ended on 30 April 1995, when the National Science Foundation ended its sponsorship of the internet backbone service and support of the internet became transferred to the various private and public internet service providers).

The next year, the ACM Hypertext '93 conference was held in Seattle, Washington, and there was still no sign of the World Wide Web anywhere in the conference program. There was, however, a table in the demonstration area where Marc Andreessen of the National Centre for Supercomputing Applications (NCSA) of the University of Illinois Urbana-Champaign was demonstrating a browser for the World Wide Web which he had made available in September 1993. It was called Mosaic and displayed documents with embedded graphics and various typefaces.

I was immediately struck by how effective this was, and how it was very likely that this was the start of something significant – it looked like the 'railway' revolution' was arriving at last.

While I was in Seattle I popped in to see my old friends at InfoAccess Inc. and strongly suggested that they should ensure that these Web technologies figured heavily in their future product plans.

Mosaic was an instant success, from an initial 5,000 copies per month, by mid-1994 they were shipping over 50,000 copies each month. Mosaic later became the foundation for not only Netscape, but also the Opera, Firefox and Microsoft's Internet Explorer browsers.

As the NCSA was a publicly funded research body, they didn't have to worry about the commercial prospects for what they developed, but Andreessen quickly left the NCSA and teamed up with the founder of Silicon Graphics, Jim Clark, to form a new company called Netscape to quickly build a fully commercial Web browser. Together they made a trip back to Illinois and hired many of the key engineers from the NCSA to create their product.

Netscape, more than anything else, turned the World Wide Web into the standard system for online publishing and set it on the path to world domination.

21

THE WEB TAKES OFF

Back in 1992 in Milan I had been asked if I would host the next European ACM Hypertext conference in Edinburgh in September 1994. I had agreed to do that mostly because I knew that, although I couldn't affect the selection of the peer-reviewed technology presentations, I would have the ability to choose my own keynote speakers.

The conference was held on 18th–23rd September 1994 during an unseasonable Indian summer heat wave. We kitted out the venerable Assembly Rooms, right in the middle of Edinburgh's New Town, which had been the principal gathering place for Edinburgh's events ever since it was first built in George Street back in 1787. It really wasn't ideal for a modern technology conference but, rather frustratingly, the new Edinburgh International Conference Centre wasn't to open until the year after.

I invited, and was delighted that they had all accepted, my dream team of keynote speakers – Doug Engelbart, the prophet of our community; developer of the world's first practical personal computer system with hypertext features, and the inventor of the computer mouse; Jakob Nielsen, the then

preeminent expert on hypertext and human factors, later to be
described by the *New York Times* as the 'guru of web usability';
and finally Tim Berners-Lee himself, the inventor of the World
Wide Web, which by that time was just beginning to be recognised as the huge force that it was later to become.

Doug Engelbart opened the conference by telling us his
own fascinating story. Back in 1945, Doug had been a 20-year-
old US Navy radar technician when, as I've recounted, he read
'As We May Think' by Vannevar Bush in *The Atlantic*, in a Red
Cross library in the Philippines. Later, in 1962 when he was at
the Stanford Research Institute in Palo Alto, he wrote a letter to
Bush as part of an application for support for his project to
build a prototype version of Bush's proposed Memex information navigation system, which he called oN Line System (NLS).

Doug Engelbart at ECHT94

Doug had demonstrated this system at the Fall 1968 Joint
Computer Conference in his famous 'Mother of All Demos'
demonstration and he showed video sequences of this event as
part of this opening keynote.

It's a really impressive demonstration even today; it was a graphics-based system, driven by a five-key chord keyboard and the world's first computer mouse, and he navigated through pages of information, text and graphics, all interconnected by hyperlinks, which were triggered by pointing and clicking on the embedded buttons with the mouse.

The hypertext community universally recognise this as the first ever implementation of a hypertext system and it was fascinating to hear from Doug the background to his demonstration, including his description of the phenomenal cost at that time of mounting the whole thing. Doug wondered in passing why the world had adopted his computer mouse but had ignored his five-key keyboard, which he held up for us all to see; Doug had always found it to be a much better interface for text input than a full standard 'QWERTY' keyboard.

What Doug had created was the prototype of the modern personal computer. The direct descendants of his system are the Apple Mac and Microsoft Windows computers, and followed by the iPhone and the iPad.

Doug was a delightful and extremely modest man; he came to Edinburgh accompanied by his wife Ballard (who was sadly to pass away three years later). They had been married for 47 years and had four children. We invited them to our home for dinner and they accepted. It was such a privilege to meet and spend time with the man who had done so much to invent the means that we would all access and share information in the future but, as with many of the truly great innovators, including Tim Berners-Lee, he had never become personally wealthy, unlike the many Silicon Valley entrepreneurs who later fully exploited these technologies.

Jakob Nielsen, then with SunSoft, was already measuring usability on the internal Web at Sun Microsystems, where at that time the number of WWW servers was doubling every 56 days. He spoke on the subject 'Too Much Hypertext, or too

Little' and argued that hypertext links needed to be used sparingly, and other user interface techniques, such as icons to aid navigation, should be used more. He particularly criticised Apple's eWorld, which had recently been launched. This displayed a three-dimensional model of a town with various buildings representing the 'Learning Centre', the 'Library', the 'Info Station' and so on. This, argued Nielsen, was ridiculously complex: interfaces should be as simple as possible, and there was nothing wrong with text as a descriptor.

Jakob was later to set up a business with usability expert Don Norman to form the Nielsen Norman consultancy, and they became the leading experts on subjects such as 'coping with information overload' and 'navigating large information spaces'. Although there were several papers on the technology streams of the conference on usability issues, Jakob was the one who addressed the issue in a systematic and comprehensive manner.

Of course, Tim Berners-Lee has since become one of the best-known computer scientists in the world – he has been knighted, won the Queen Elizabeth Prize for Engineering, the James Clerk Maxwell Award, the Turing Award, and lots of others. He even featured in person in the Opening Ceremony of the 2012 London Olympics.

But back in 1994 only a few of us knew Tim; the hypertext community at this conference was very aware that his simple, uncomplicated link system, running on top of the internet, was gathering huge momentum. Some saw it as too simplistic to be interesting, but it was this simplicity that ultimately led to its success.

Although Berners-Lee had developed the Web at CERN, and it had become a recognised project there, he really needed to leave for it to succeed – CERN was a particle physics research facility and not the best place to pioneer computer science research.

Time Berners-Lee at ECHT94

On 30th April 1993, CERN gave up any ownership claims to the World Wide Web, putting it into the public domain and opening it up to be used and developed, royalty-free, by anyone.

In late summer 1994, Berners-Lee moved his work and Web advocacy to the MIT in Cambridge Massachusetts and started the World Wide Web Consortium (W3C) – it was clear that in order for his vision of the global Web to survive, some neutral body was needed to build consensus among the various forces that were pulling the Web in different directions.

At the ECHT94 conference, Tim was optimistic about the benefits to humanity that widespread adoption of his World Wide Web would enable, but when I asked him where he thought the biggest threat would come from, he was clear. It was the major software publishers of this world – Microsoft and its ilk – that he thought to be a threat to open standards.

Naturally, software companies always try to capture markets for their proprietary environments and are averse to shared standards; if they can somehow become their own de-facto standard (as with Microsoft Windows or Microsoft Office), there are, of course, huge commercial benefits. Tim also criticised the development of closed 'apps' which, although built on top of WWW architecture, are not searchable or reachable on the open Web.

In *Weaving the Web*, Tim wrote about this time:

> *No sooner had I arrived at MIT than I was off to Edinburgh, Scotland, for the next European Conference on Hypermedia Technology. It was run by Ian Ritchie of Owl, whom I had tried to convince four years earlier to develop a Web browser as part of Owl's hypertext product, Guide. It was here that I saw Doug Engelbart show the video of his original NLS system. Despite the Web's rise, the SGML community was still criticizing HTML as an inferior subset, and proposing that the Web rapidly adopt all of SGML. Others felt that HTML should be disconnected from the ungainly SGML world and kept clean and simple.*
>
> *Dale Dougherty of O'Reilly Associates, who had gathered the early Web creators at the first Wizards workshop and other meetings, saw a third alternative. After one session at the conference, a bunch of us adjourned to a local pub. As we were sitting around on stools nursing our beer glasses, Dale started telling everyone that, in essence, the SGML community was passé and that HTML would end up stronger. He felt we didn't have to accept the SGML world wholesale or ignore it. Quietly, with a smile, Dale began saying, 'We can change it.' He kept repeating the phrase, like a mantra. 'We can change it.'*

I had arranged with the Scotch Malt Whisky Society to organise a whisky-tasting session after our conference programme was over for the day, with three distinct types of whisky being offered – a lowland, a highland and an island – each of which exhibited different flavour characteristics. Thus, the two key pioneers of our world, Doug Engelbart and Tim Berners-Lee, were able to meet and bond in Edinburgh over a few glasses of excellent Scotch.

The very next month, October 1994, Netscape, who had recruited many of the NCSA Mosaic team, released the first version of its browser, dubbed Mozilla. It was a beta (test) version, released so people could try it and send suggestions for any improvements. As he had with Mosaic, Andreessen pumped out the message about Mozilla over the newsgroups, and users snapped it up.

From that day on, the World Wide Web, initially using browsers from Mosaic and Netscape but later with other browsers, including when Microsoft released their Internet Explorer, bundled free with Windows, it was to go on to flatten all competitors.

The World Wide Web was ready to take over the world.

22

CONCLUSION

L ooking back over our experiences over this period, it had been a truly fascinating and exhilarating time that we had lived through.

The 1980s had been the key decade when the personal computer began to emerge as the fundamental information tool for all business – and many personal – needs. Although the Apple II had been launched in 1976, it really took off with the launch of the iconic IBM PC in 1981 and Apple Mac in 1984 and created the opportunity for the development of new software solutions to make it simpler to operate what were, initially, fundamentally quite complex machines.

Initially there had been scepticism about whether many executives would have their own personal computer, most expected their assistants to continue to do the administrative tasks. But the development of a novel range of easy-to-use applications, such as spreadsheets, graphics, and presentation tools, led most executives to choose to interact directly with their own means of communication using their personal computers.

The development of graphic user interface (GUI) systems

and the arrival of highly useable affordable computers led by the Apple Mac began the move to a form of computing that could more easily be used by anyone.

Although we had been convinced, rightly, that this form of computing would eventually become standard it did take some considerable time to happen. Even though it was launched in 1986 it wasn't until version 3.0 of Microsoft Windows in 1990 that the mass of computer users started to switch to working with these easy-to-use graphically based environments. Even the computer industry has difficulty with change.

Over the succeeding years, computers began to be better able to manage images and access network communications, initially via relatively slow connections – 2400 bits per second being typical – and at that time there was no universal email system; people were forced to use private dial-up services such as CompuServe or America Online (AOL), both of which were consumer focussed rather than business oriented.

When the internet finally became available to all in the mid-1990s many users found that email was the 'killer app' which encouraged them to use their computer more intensively. They also bought the new laptop computers, which could be packed in a briefcase, which were by then beginning to come on to the market so that they could stay in touch wherever they were.

The arrival of the World Wide Web, on the back of the internet, created an attractive and powerful method of accessing a huge amount of information although initially quite limited in performance capability. For some time, they weren't capable of playing video sequences, or accessing the internet at reasonable speed. It typically took many seconds or even minutes to download individual images.

It wasn't until the beginning of the twenty-first century that computers finally became the highly effective information

machines that they are today, and broadband and mobile telephony began to offer better data connectivity.

The power and connectivity of such devices led to the
arrival of the iPhone in 2007 and the iPad in 2010. At last, the
Dynabook concept that Alan Kay predicted back in 1972 was
available to all. The ultimate online information machine. The
real 'personal computer' – one that you could, indeed, hold
above your head.

BACK IN THE 1980S, when the world of the personal computer
was emerging, my colleagues and I found ourselves with the
once-in-a-lifetime opportunity of making a key contribution to
designing the future of these information machines. It was one
that we seized enthusiastically.

At OWL, for six years in the 1980s, we developed the technology behind a highly sophisticated world-leading system for
the delivery of massive quantities of information in all sorts of
formats, from data tables to technical manuals, to images and
even integrated video sequences. Our hypertext system would
work over networks.

Of course, we weren't the only ones. Other systems, like
ZOG, FRESS, Intermedia, Notecards, Xanadu and Hypercard
were also developing solutions to the effective delivery of interactive information.

In retrospect, the analogy that I used in my keynote speech
at ECHT in 1992 seems to have been confirmed by events. Our
efforts, and others in the hypertext community, were the equivalent of the technologies that were invented to enable the canal
age – the engineering techniques that went on to build the
railway age's bridges, vehicles, tunnels, stations and so on.

When, in 1994, the World Wide Web arrived, like the railways, it flattened all before it; we early hypertext 'canal operators' became mostly redundant.

At OWL, we had thought we were designing how people everywhere would access their information. We were, but we were undoubtedly servicing only the early adopter market. To a large extent, we did lead the way. The pioneering work done at OWL set the scene for the hypertext revolution to come.

The reason that Tim Berners-Lee's World Wide Web took off so spectacularly in the mid-1990s was that it provided a very simple universal mechanism for connecting information over the internet, without much of the publishing enabling technology complexity that had troubled the hypertext researchers. And this all happened exactly at the point that the internet became free and open to all, along with the arrival of NCSA's Mosaic browser.

A truly serendipitous set of circumstances.

23

KEY TIMELINES

- June 1973 – graduated with BSc Hons (2.1) in Computer Science, Heriot-Watt University
- July 1973 – started work at ICL Dalkeith
- March 1982 – meeting to transfer PERQ project to new management
- January 1983 – CPM83 conference in San Francisco
- July 1983 – News received that ICL was planning to close Dalkeith research centre.
- December 1983 – established partnership at Office Workstations Ltd based at borrowed office at University of Edinburgh Bush Estate
- June 1984 – Incorporation of Office Workstations Limited
- June 1984 – Initial meeting with Professor Peter Brown at University of Kent in Canterbury
- October 1984 – First phase of investment by Scottish Development Agency, Investors in Industry (3i) and Candover of £125,000. £50,000 from founders.
- October 1984 – Established first office at Abbeymount Techbase

- 10th September 1986 – launch of Guide for the Apple Macintosh
- October 1986 – meeting with Philip s to discuss CD-I
- April 1987 – first meeting at Renault with IBM
- 21st May 1987 – First version of Guide for IBM PCs running Windows
- June 1987 – Visit to IBM Winchester and U of Southampton
- 20th July 1987 – Apple Cupertino meeting to brief us about Hypercard
- October 1987 – Meeting at Microrim
- November 1987 – emergency refinancing
- 28th January 1988 – meeting at Apple to resolve HyperCard issue
- February 1988 – meeting at Boca Raton – IBM Renault thru Feb March
- April 1988 – launch of French Guide at George V Hotel, Paris
- May 1988- Strategy session at Airth Castle
- August 1988 – fist approach from Yamaichi
- October 1988 – DTS CD-Word meeting
- October 1988 – BCS Awards London
- November 1988 – Visit to OWL by Ted Nelson
- February 1989 – Initial meeting at OWL with Matsushita executives
- June 1989 – Meeting in London with Matsushita to agree terms
- August 1989 – Further meeting with Matsushita to finalise terms
- December 1989 – Completion meeting for Matsushita to acquire OWL.
- November 1992 – ACM Hypertext conference in Milan (ECHT92)

- November 1993 – ACM Hypertext conference in
  Seattle at which Mark Andreesen demonstrated the
  Mosaic browser for the World Wide Web.
- September 1994 – ACM Hypertext conference in
  Edinburgh. Keynote speakers include Doug
  Engelbart and Tim Berners-Lee.
- October 1994 – World Wide Web consortium (W3C)
  established at MIT.
- October 1994 – Resigned as CEO of OWL

24

GLOSSARY

- **3RCC** – Three Rivers Computer Corporation. The Pittsburgh company which brought the Perq to market, based on designs from Carnegie-Mellon University.
- **ACM** – The Association for Computer Machinery. The leading international institute for computer research, headquartered in New York.
- **AI** – Artificial Intelligence. The research field which attempts to emulate the analysis and decision-making abilities of humans.
- **BBC Micro** – an early British personal computer which was the basis of an educational drive to teach computing skills led by the BBC.
- **Bot** – an automated piece of computer code that works on demand, such as at a certain time.
- **BTG** – British Technology Group. The body that originally had the rights to exploit any publicly funded research spinning out of UK Universities or research institutes. It later lost the automatic right

but continued to commercially exploit research developments from academia..

- **CERN** – the multi-national research centre near Geneva where the world's physicists conduct experiments in particle science by enabling collisions of basic particles.
- **CMU** – Carnegie-Mellon University. The engineering-oriented university based in Pittsburgh known for advanced computer science research.
- **Compiler** – Applications which convert programming languages into machine compatible versions which can then be run on computers.
- **Courseware** – software applications designed to support the teaching of a class.
- **Desktop Publishing** – the name given to the system for the creation of sophisticated documents, pioneered by Aldus Pagemaker running on an Apple Macintosh and printing via Apple's LaserWriter.
- **DPI** – The number of 'dots per inch' – a measure of the resolution of computer graphics. Above 300 DPI is regarded as a level of image quality that looks reasonably natural to the naked eye.
- **Firmware** – pieces of internal software which enable a particular task inside a computer, like driving a peripheral.
- **Gaijins** – A Japanese word for a non-Japanese person
- **GUI** – Graphics User Interface. The format of all modern personal computers based on overlapping or exchangeable windows of high-quality presentations of rich data, with a selection device such as a touch screen or mouse.

- **HML** – Hypertext Markup Language. Our variant of SGML which adds tags for hypertext elements such as hypertext pointers and targets, stretch text elements and their contents, and notes.
- **HTML** – the SGML variant which underpins the World Wide Web.
- **HyperCard** – a program launched by Apple Computer in August 1987 which was marketed as a hypertext product (although its developer had intended it to be an application development tool).
- **LaserDisk** – devices for storage of larger quantities of information such as video sequences.
- **Mouse** – a computer accessory which enables the user to point and select objects on a computer screen.
- **MU5** – an innovative micro-coded computer developed at the University of Manchester, famed for computer design. The MU5 became the basis for the ICL 2900 series of computers.
- **NDA** – Non-disclosure agreement. A legal agreement to hold secret any information that has been provided, normally to protect trade or commercial secrets from wider distribution.
- **NeXT** – the advanced graphics workstation that was developed by the company that Steve Jobs formed after his dismissal from Apple.
- **OEM** – Original Equipment Manufacturer: a company that obtains and resells components acquired from third party developers rather than developing these in-house.
- **Operating Systems (OS)** – the permanent software platform on which applications run.
- **Pascal** – a computer language. In this context the original PERQ was designed as a Pascal-based

machine which was somewhat unusual and made it
difficult to run standard software which was
increasingly being written to run the more standard
Unix environment.

- **Postscript** – a computing language developed by
John Warnock and Chuck Geschke at Adobe which
defines the basic elements of a printed document
such as typefaces and graphic elements for a high
resolution printer such as a laser printer.
- **RAL** – Rutherford Appleton Laboratory. The unit
within the UK's research funding council which was
responsible for computer science research strategy
in the 1980s.
- **SBDS** – Service Bay Diagnostic System. A project
led by Hewlett-Packard to create online manuals for
automobile servicing commissioned by the Ford
Motor corporation. OWL was contacted to provide
the document management of this system.
- **SDA** – Scottish Development Agency. The strategic
economic development unit of the Scottish
Government. In 1991 the organisation was
restructured to create Scottish Enterprise.
- **SDF** – Scottish Development Finance. The
investment division of the Scottish Development
Agency.
- **SGML** - Standard Generalized Markup Language is
a metadata standard for how to specify a document
markup language. It defines non-printed 'tags'
which indicate the elements of a document
(headlines, sub-heads, captions, references etc.) so
they can be interpreted later when the document is
displayed or printed.
- **SPICE** – (Software Process Improvement and
Capability dEtermination) the advanced distributed

operating system research project based at
Carnegie-Mellon University.

- **SSHF** – Scottish Software House Federation. The
new trade association set up to represent Scotland's
software industry. The name was subsequently
shortened to 'Scottish Software Federation' and then
later changed to 'ScotlandIS'.
- **Unix** – an open standard operating system which is
widely used on personal computers.
- **VGA** – a technology to drive a high resolution
display screen.
- **VisiCalc** – the first spreadsheet, developed for the
Apple II. One of the early 'killer apps' – programs
which alone justify the purchase of a computer.
- **W3C** – World Wide Web consortium. The body that
determines standards used in the World Wide Web.
- **XML** – a development of HTML which also defines
content elements within documents, allowing data
to be more easily shared between systems.

ABOUT THE AUTHOR

Ian Ritchie is Chairman of Tern plc (AIM: TERN), Computer Application Services Ltd., and Krotos Ltd. He was Chairman of iomart Group plc from 2008 until 2018. He is a board member of Edinburgh's Royal Lyceum Theatre, and the Scottish Council for Development and Industry (SCDI).

Ritchie founded and managed Office Workstations Limited (OWL) in Edinburgh in 1984 and its subsidiary OWL International Inc in Seattle from 1985. OWL became the first and largest supplier of Hypertext/Hypermedia authoring tools (a forerunner to the World Wide Web) for personal computers based on its Guide product. OWL's customers used its systems to implement large interactive multimedia documentation systems in industry sectors such as automobile, defence, publishing, finance, and education. OWL was sold to Panasonic of Japan in December 1989.

He was Honorary Treasurer of the Royal Academy of Engineering from 2012 to 2016 and Vice President of the Royal Society of Edinburgh from 2012 to 2016. Ritchie has also been active in venture capital as a director of Northern Venture Trust plc from 1997 to 2001 and as a member of the advisory board of Pentech Ventures from 2001 to 2016. He was a founding director, and Chairman (1988-1990), of the Scottish Software Federation (now ScotlandIS).

Ritchie was awarded a CBE in the 2003 New Years Honours list for services to enterprise and education. He is a Fellow and a past-President of the British Computer Society (1998-99), and was a member of Scotland's Cultural Commission in 2005/06.

He has a BSc Hons. in Computer Science from Heriot-Watt University (1973), and was awarded Honorary Doctorates by Heriot-Watt University in July 2000, the Robert Gordon University in July 2001, the University of Abertay Dundee in June 2002, and the University of Edinburgh in December 2003.

He served as Chairman of Judges for the Scottish Young Software Engineer awards from 1989 until 2019. He has also been a judge on the joint UK Research Councils Business Plan awards, the Economist Innovation awards, Converge Challenge, and the Royal Academy of Engineering MacRoberts' Awards. He currently acts as a judge in the Spectator Disruptive Business award.

He has been the Founding Chairman of Voxar Ltd, VIS Entertainment plc, Orbital Software Group plc, Digital Bridges Ltd. and Sonaptic Ltd. He was a trustee of Bletchley Park from (1999 -2009), a board member of Scottish Enterprise (1999-2005), the Particle Physics and Astronomy Research Council (PPARC 1999-2003), the Scottish Higher and Further Education Funding Council (SFC, 2002-07), Channel 4 Television Corporation (2000-05), and EPIC Group plc. (1999-2005), the UK's leading e-learning company.

He is the author of 'New Media Publishing - Opportunities

from the digital revolution' published by Financial Times Telecoms and Media Publishing (1996).

His TED talk has been viewed over 650,000 times.

Printed in Great Britain
by Amazon

32232174R00136